Junior naturalist

AT THE SEASHORE

WRITTEN BY
KEN HOY

ILLUSTRATED BY
ADRIAN RIGBY

DESIGNED BY
GRAHAM BROWN

WARD LOCK

First Published in Great Britain by
Ward Lock Limited, 8 Clifford Street,
Mayfair, London W1. 1986

© Brown Wells and Jacobs Limited, London. 1986

Written by Ken Hoy
Illustrations by Adrian Rigby
Designed by Graham Brown
Typesetting by Words & Pictures Limited
Colour Originated by RCS Graphics Limited
Printed and Bound by Henri Proost & CIE PVBA.

British Library Cataloguing in Publication Data

Hoy, Ken
    Junior naturalist at the seashore.
    1. Seashore biology—Great Britain
    —Juvenile literature
    I. Title   II. Rigby, Adrian
    574.941   QH137

ISBN 0-7063-6438-4

CONTENTS

HIGH TIDE – LOW TIDE: Why the seashore is the most varied of habitats for everything that lives there. 4–5

SEA-WATER & TIDES: How tides are caused and why the sea is salt. Measuring and checking the tides. 6–7

MAKING WAVES: How they are caused and what they do. Some of the ways in which sea-water is different. 8–9

ROCKS, SAND & MUD: The way the sea and its waves affect and change the land and the coastline. Clues to look for to see what is happening. 10–11

AERIAL FEEDERS: Seabirds that spend most of the time flying in order to search for food. How to recognise different gulls. 12–13

UNDERWATER HUNTERS: Seabirds that feed below the surface of the sea. Watching seabirds flying and feeding. 14–15

WALKING FEEDERS: Birds that feed on the shore and how to watch them. 16–17

SEASONS & TIDES: The tidal and seasonal movements and migrations of birdlife on the coast. How and what to record. 18–19

SEASHORE FISH: The kinds of fish that you can expect to see in the pools and those that come in with the tide. How to "watch" the pools. 20–21

SURVIVAL PROBLEMS: The difficulties involved in surviving on the different types of seashore. Where to search to find things. 22–23

CRUSTY CHARACTERS: The crabs, shrimps and prawns and their relatives. Nets and other equipment needed to explore the shore. 24–25

FLOWER ANIMALS: Sea anemones, jelly-fish and star-fish that you might find. How to see and examine them. 26–27

BUILDERS & BURROWERS: The various worms that live in mud, sand and rocks. How to start a marine aquarium. 28–29

SEA SNAILS: The seashell creatures with one foot. What to keep in a marine aquarium and how to feed them. 30–31

TWIN SHELLS: The bi-valve shellfish – cockles and mussels and many others. Making a shell collection. 32–33

SEA SOUP: How to see the small, almost microscopic, plants and animals – the plankton – and some of the strange creatures that feed on them. 34–35

SEAWEEDS: The common seaweeds and the zones on the shore that they occupy. How to preserve seaweeds and record the life of the shore. 36–37

SEASHORE PLANTS: The "land" plants that survive in the dunes or salt marshes and how to examine some of them. 38–39

TIDE-LINE DETECTIVE: Living creatures and the remains of plants and animals that are washed up by the tide. What to look for. 40–41

SEASHORE MAMMALS: Seals, porpoises, dolphins and whales. Stones and fossils that may be found on the beach. 42–43

THE MESSY MAMMAL: What man has done and is doing to the sea, the shore and the coastline. What you can do to improve matters. 44–45

SEASHORE CODE, some useful addresses and Index. 46–47–48

HIGH TIDE – LOW TIDE

TIDE-IN

Prawn

Common Blenny

Acorn Barnacles

Winkles

When you visit the beach whatever you do will depend upon one thing – is the tide 'in' or 'out'?

It is even more important for the plants and creatures that live there. It may be true to say that no other place where living things exist, no other *habitat*, changes so drastically or so quickly.

Think about a shellfish such as a Limpet – it is not a fish but a mollusc, a relation of snails and slugs. The limpet lives half way down the beach on a rock, perhaps partly covered with seaweed. Every six hours waves batter it for a while. Then it has perhaps five hours under the cold salty sea water to crawl about feeding before more waves crash over it again, then it is in the air – no water, just a hot sun drying everything up.

During this time an oyster catcher, or a human being, may come along and try to dislodge it from its rock. If it is winter time it will not be the blazing sun but an icy wind trying to dry it up. Some six hours later back come the waves again.

What a strange life? Think of what it is

necessary to do or to have to survive in such a strange place.

The same changing conditions apply to the worms in the sand, to the shrimps and fishes in the rock pools. They must get back to their pool before the tide leaves them. The sea weeds on the rocks and breakwaters are also affected. They must survive in the hot sun without drying up.

Sea birds like waders or gulls can feed on the mud or sand banks when the tide is out but as it comes in again they must retreat up the beach and finally find somewhere else to go until the shore is exposed again.

There are only a certain number of hours when it is possible to feed on the wet sand or mud and a number of those hours will be at night. Therefore feeding must go on in the dark as well.

The tide, then, is more important than whether it is day or night.

If you are a creature living near the low tide mark you will be under the water nearly all the time, perhaps only in the air for an hour or two. On the other hand if you live at the

TIDE-OUT

Turnstone

Shore Crab

top of the beach you will be battered by waves for an hour or so and then dried by the hot sun for 10 or 11 hours.

Every creature will have its enemies too. There will be enemies for the worm when the tide is 'in' – fish and crabs; there will be different enemies when the tide is 'out' – gulls, wading birds and even fishermen digging for bait. Different means of protection or hiding or defence are required each time.

It can be worse; besides the salt sea water, fresh rain water, hot sun, drying winds, icy temperatures and battering waves, a shore creature may be washed away by the current, buried in sand or suffocated in mud.

The tidal movement of the sea is very important, then, and makes a great difference to everything that lives within reach of the tide.

To study the variety of life that lives on the seashore we must know something about the tide and why and how it occurs, about the waves and what they do, and about the rocks, stones, sand and mud that make up the beaches.

DO YOU KNOW

- There are mountain ranges, even volcanoes and deep valleys in the floor of the sea. The deepest valley or trench is in the Pacific near Japan and it is deeper than Mount Everest is tall. 10,000 metres or over 30,000 ft deep.
- The biggest range of mountains in the world is a mile under the Atlantic Ocean. It is called the Mid Atlantic Ridge, is 10,000 miles long and up to 500 miles wide. Its mountains rise an average of 10,000 ft or over 3,000 metres above the sea bed.
- The Mediterranean Sea, which is almost cut off from other oceans, has very little tidal change at all.
- There are 7,000 miles or 11,000 kilometres of coastline around the British Isles.
- Giant waves that have been called 'tidal waves' (although nothing to do with tides) are created by earthquakes. They are giant ripples that are sent through the ocean for thousands of miles and can travel at 400 miles per hour, with as much as 90 miles between each 'ripple'. They only reach a great height – as much as 50 ft or 16 metres – when they reach shallower water.
- In the middle of the North Sea is a shallow area which was land covered by forest only a few thousand years ago. It is only 60 ft or 18 metres below the surface and sometimes pieces of what were trees are trawled up by fishing boats. Part of this area is called the Dogger Bank by fishermen.

SEA-WATER AND TIDES

Seas and oceans cover much of the world's surface. Only just over a quarter is land. On the land there is more water – lakes, reservoirs, ponds, rivers and streams – and this water comes from rain and snow. This *fresh-water* is different from the water in the seas; sea water is salty as mineral salts washed from the land are constantly being carried to the sea by rivers and concentrated there because for millions of years the oceans have been 'drying-up' but leaving the salt behind.

As water is warmed it 'dries-up' or evaporates into the air as an invisible gas called *water vapour*. Puddles, ponds, streams, rivers, the seas and oceans are always drying up, that is giving up water vapour into the air.

Warm air differs from cold air in two important ways. As it becomes warmer it expands and becomes slightly lighter, and therefore rises above cold air. Secondly, warm air can hold a greater amount of water vapour. As water vapour rises in the air farther and farther from the ground it becomes cooler and the invisible water vapour must turn back into microscopic droplets of water and, like the hot 'steam' from a kettle, becomes visible as a mist. Then we call it clouds. The clouds

gather more and more water droplets, these join together and eventually become so heavy they must fall as rain. The rain that falls on the land then begins washing out more salts to the sea. The water has followed a circular process – this is called the *water cycle*.

Besides the water being salty we have already noticed something else happening on the shore – the tide has come in or gone out! What really has happened is the level of the sea in your part of the world has risen at that time. What causes it to happen? The gravitational pull of the moon 'pulls' the ocean water towards that side of the Earth facing the moon. However, it has *also* pulled the Earth itself more than the oceans on the other side which have tended to be 'left behind'. This means high tides occur at the same time on the side nearest the moon *and* on the side farthest away. (See diagram)

The Sun, although much farther away than the Moon, also helps a little. When the Sun and Moon are pulling together *or* whether the Sun is helping pull the tide on the opposite side then the high tides are even higher. These very high tides are called *Spring tides* (a confusing name which has nothing to do with

Oyster Catchers

Eider

Herring Gull

Purple Sandpiper

TIDE WATCH

When you are by the sea it is always important to find out the time of high and low tides. So much of what you can or cannot do or see depends upon the tide. Check the changes each day.

- Look in a diary to find the state of the Moon and then see whether the high tide is decreasing or increasing up the beach with each tide each day.
- Look for the different high tide lines – **strand lines**, where the floating debris – **flotsam**, has been left behind. Sometimes a strong wind will also affect the height of the tide.
- At a harbour side or quay-side you may see a marked board in the water which shows the rise and fall of tides as the depth of water. Try

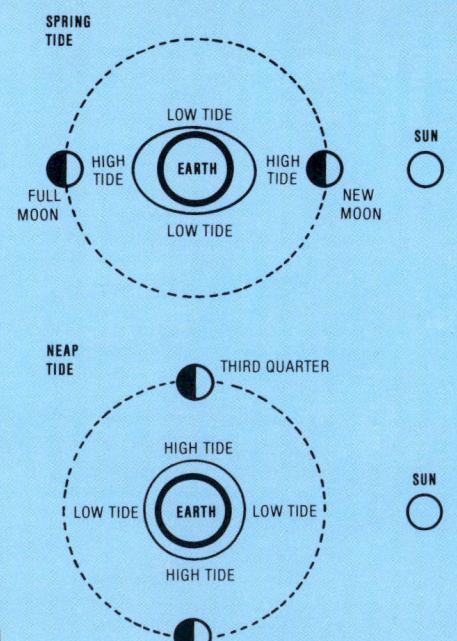

to work out the difference between the highest **Spring** high tide and the lowest **Neap** high tide – seven days later.

- When at the seaside the sky and the weather are more noticeable and important to us. Notice, when the weather is settled, that more clouds form as the day goes on; they usually form over the land which is warmer than the sea. Can you work out why?
- Notice also after a still, calm summer morning that by the afternoon there is a wind blowing, usually from the sea towards the land. In the evening as the sun goes and the land cools, does the wind drop? Can you work out what has been happening?
- Although a common belief, the Moon and the tides have no effect on general weather patterns.

the season). However, when the Sun is pulling to one side it is lessening the pull by the Moon and the high tides are not quite so high. These are the *Neap tides*. Because the Moon moves around the Earth in 28 days the Neap tides and Spring tides follow a cycle which recurs every 2 weeks. Spring tides occur about the time of full moon and the new moon, while the Neap tides occur when the Moon is showing about half of its surface.

As the Earth revolves every 24 hours the high tides move around the world like two great 'waves' and there is thus a high tide every 12 hours. But because the Moon has itself moved round a little the time period is actually 12 hours and 25 minutes on average.

Currents in the oceans, around islands, through narrow channels and seas separated from the large oceans affect the tides so that they occur faster or slower in different places.

This applies to the British Isles particularly and is why a high tide varies from place to place.

Ringed Plover

Shelduck

Oyster Catcher

Redshank

MAKING WAVES

Blacktailed Godwit

Sanderling

Redshank

Day and night there are always waves breaking on the shore and they never seem to stop. Sometimes they are large, rough and powerful waves and sometimes just hardly more than smooth ripples. Wind is the cause of waves. When the sea is rough and a strong wind is blowing this fact may be obvious. But sometimes when there is no wind there are still small rippling waves that are so lazy they hardly seem to have the strength to *break*. These can be caused by wind on the sea hundreds of miles away. The greater the

SEA WATER

Sea water contains more than just common salt. There are more than ten other chemical salts which, although only present in small quantities, are very important for the life that lives in the sea.

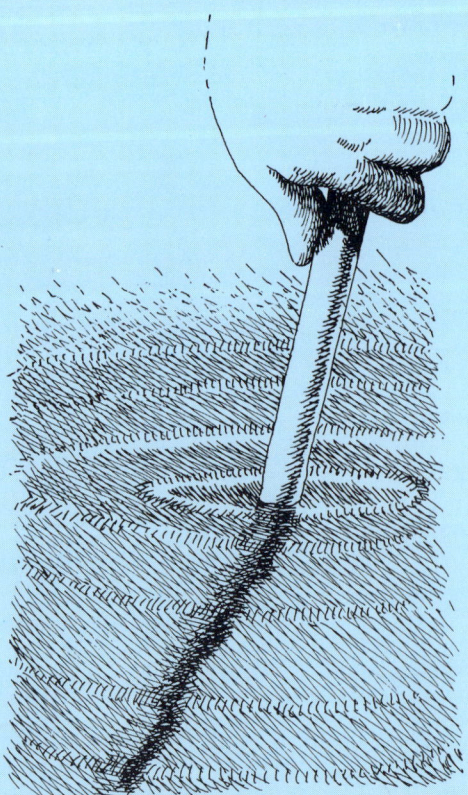

- Have you noticed how quickly cuts and scratches heal when you are bathing in the sea regularly? Sea water is a disinfectant. Notice how it stings, how it feels slimy and how, because salt attracts dampness, anything, once moistened by sea water, quickly becomes damp and sticky again. Soap will not lather in sea water.
- Because the salts in the sea make sea water slightly more dense ('thicker') than fresh water, it is more **buoyant**. Ships using fresh and salt water have different loading levels because of this difference.
- Greater evaporation concentrates the salt level – the **salinity**. The Mediterranean Sea, because it is nearly enclosed, is slightly more salty than elsewhere. The Dead Sea, which dries up rapidly in the heat, is much lower than the sea level around the world, and is also very salty and **buoyant** – it is easy to float in it.
- Have you noticed how deceptive water is? The bottom is much farther away than it looks. It also 'bends' light. Push a stick or cane at an angle into a pool of water and the part in the water will appear to be at a different angle.
- Have you observed how the colour of the sea changes? Sometimes this is caused by mud or sand, sometimes by minerals, certainly it varies with the depth of the water, but the main reason is the light reflected from the sky.
- Look at the many colours different artists have seen in sea scenes that they have painted. Try mixing some of the colours you can see – it might be easier than trying to find the right words to describe them.

Blackhead Gull (juvenile)

Ringed Plover

stretch of sea the wind can blow across the greater the size, speed and violence of an ocean roller.

The distance between one wave and the next is called the *length* of the wave. The greater the length the greater the speed. The *height* of a wave is the vertical difference between the top or *crest* of the wave and the bottom of the valley or *trough* between the waves.

Waves are not what they seem when they break on the beach. Only as they reach the shallow beach does the water move forward, elsewhere in deep water waves are like a ripple passing *through* the water. Watch something floating on the sea – a gull – it merely rises and falls as the wave goes by. Watch waves made by the wind blowing across a field of grass or corn!

It is only as the water becomes shallow that the bottom of the wave starts to 'drag' along sand or shingle and is slowed down while the top of the wave travels on and finally overbalances and crashes forward, shooting up the beach. This part of the water is called the *swash*. When the swash runs out of strength and runs back it is called the *back-wash*.

Watch a ball, or better still, an orange, which is heavier and will not be affected by the wind, in the swash and back-wash; sometimes it

merely goes back and forth. But if the waves are approaching the beach at an angle the orange goes up the beach in the same direction as the wave but travels in the back-wash straight down the beach. The next swash then washes it up at an angle again. Let this go on several times and then think about the fact that this happens to every pebble and grain of sand. If the beach has breakwaters or *groynes* look to see if there is a difference between the beach on one side compared with the other.

What do you think the groynes do?

Sometimes there is a *tidal drift* along the shore. Moving one way as the tide is *flowing* or *flooding*, that is, coming in, and moving back the other way as the tide *ebbs* or goes out. Check this by throwing a piece of wood beyond where the waves are beginning to break and watch what happens (take care no-one is bathing!). Along some shores there are prevailing currents which tend to carry beach material more or less in one direction most of the time.

When there are strong waves hitting a sea wall or harbour wall, you will notice that they rebound and meet the next wave coming in. Watch what happens, remembering that a wave is a large moving *ripple* and the water itself does not move forward.

ROCKS, SAND AND MUD

The beaches and the coastal landscape are constantly changing. The sea never stops altering the land.

The waves battering against the land have caused cliffs to form and these waves are breaking all the year.

In storms and in winter each wave is hurling tons of water at the cliff-face. At the same time the water is also forcing and compressing air into hollows and cracks in the rock. Much of the booming noise is caused by the sudden release of trapped air.

The waves have other weapons. They are hurling rocks and stones each time, and they are also blasting the cliffs and grinding away with millions of grains of sand. From a safe place, watch the waves on a stormy day.

The rock of the cliff is also under attack from the weather as water freezing and expanding in cracks is shattering the rock itself. Gravity assists as the broken pieces fall to the foot of the cliff. The sea is then provided with more missiles which are gradually broken up and worn down. Rocks become round pebbles, pebbles become shingle which is worn into grains of sand.

All this material around our coast is available for use by the sea. In some places it is used destructively to batter the land but in other places where there are no cliffs it is thrown up into beaches and banks which in fact protect the land from wave attack. This is especially true of pebble and shingle banks. As the wave breaks and the *swash* sweeps forward large pebbles are thrown or rolled higher up the beach. The wave, having lost its energy, leaves them and retreats by disappearing down between the stones and by trickling backwards down the beach again. But when retreating, it does not have the energy to move many stones with it. The beach thus can grow higher and in fact the waves have created a barrier against which the sea crashes harmlessly.

You can watch this happening too.

If currents tend to flow along the coast in one direction more than the other, shingle and sand will be carried along too. As the waves build the beach up so the bank or *spit*, as it is called, 'grows' in the direction that the current is flowing. Often, if the coast bends away from the sea the spit continues to grow out in a straight line and a *lagoon* is formed behind the shingle bank. The tide flows gently in and out

Curlew

Saltmarsh and Lagoon

Shelduck

Sandwich Tern

Redshank

Common Tern

COASTAL DETECTIVE

Wherever you are on the coast there is a lot to be found out by simply looking and thinking.

- At low tide look at the cliffs. Are they made of soft rocks like clay, chalk, sandstone or limestone, or a hard rock like granite? If it is a rock you do not know, just decided if it is a 'hard' or a 'soft' rock that is easily worn away.
- Do the cliffs consist of one type of rock or more than one type? Is it divided into layers? This is called **stratified** and means the rock was laid down under the sea as a **sediment**. Chalk is a **sedimentary** rock but is not usually in layers. Sedimentary rocks often contain fossils.
- If there are different coloured veins running through the rock it usually means it has been subjected to great changes of heat or pressure deep underground. Sometimes, by using a lens, it is possible to see that the rock is made of tightly-packed crystals. These are rocks formed deep in the Earth.
- If there is more than one type of rock making up the cliff – has the cliff-face worn unevenly because one rock is softer?
- Examine the pebbles on the beach. Some will be the same as the nearest cliffs, but many will be quite different and could have come from miles away. Pebbles in the South West of England could have

come from Wales, Ireland or Scotland while those on the East and South East side could have come from Yorkshire, Northumbria, Scotland and even Scandinavia. Look in an atlas.
- All stones will be rounded to some extent, depending upon how long they have been rolled about by the sea. Some stones will be harder than others. Scratch one with

another to find which is the harder.
- Limestone is usually greyish and will 'fizz' if you drop a spot of vinegar on it.
- Chip one stone with another to examine the broken area for a **crystalline** structure (made up of crystals).
- Sometimes broken glass or brick is worn and its appearance changed too.

of the lagoon but, with little or no wave action, everything is washed in by the tide – the sand and mud suspended in the water is left to settle in the lagoon or *slack*. Special plants that can stand salt water grow there and their stems and roots increasingly collect and hold more mud. In this way the lagoon slowly becomes more shallow and eventually changes into salt marsh and finally dry land.

At the mouths of rivers where the current of the river meets and cancels out the force of the incoming tide, a sand or shingle bank sometimes forms. This is called a *bar*. As the tide is coming in rough choppy water will show you where the bar has been formed. Look and watch but keep away – very dangerous currents occur in such places! At low tide you may see deep ridges in the sand caused by the strong current. The stronger the current, the deeper and wider are the ridges.

Marram grass on dunes

Where beach slope is long and gentle and where the low tide mark is a long way from the land, grains of sand can be picked-up and carried in the wind if it is blowing across the drying sand at a speed of more than 10 m.p.h. or 16 k.p.h. It is in such places and conditions that sand-dunes are formed by the wind.

AERIAL FEEDERS

To many people birds at the seaside are sea-gulls – however there are different kinds of gulls and many other sea or shore birds.

It is possible to group seashore birds according to how they feed. Some walk and poke around the shore for food, some swim and take their food on the surface or under-water, others search for food mostly by flying.

Gulls should be placed in the last group – the aerial feeders. They do not walk about a great deal, usually if you see them on the ground they are resting or preening. Like many birds that spend a lot of their lives in the air, their wings are long and narrow. They are thus suited to flying in the open in strong air currents using the least amount of energy with slow wing beats and their ability to glide almost indefinitely if the wind is strong enough. Gulls might be called the crows of the sea, for like crows on land they are scavengers and they are also predatory upon eggs, young and weak or sick birds.

There are six gulls that you are likely to see by the seashore. Two have black backs and one of these, the Greater Blackbacked gull, is our largest gull having a wing-span of over 1½ metres or over 5 ft. The other is the Lesser Blackbacked gull which is a migratory gull in Britain as most others of the same species come here in the winter from Scandinavia.

The commonest of the large gulls is the pale grey backed Herring Gull. This is the gull with the loud "laughing" cry.

GULL AND TERN SPOTTING

What to look for:
The colour of the legs and their length, what is the height of bird when resting?
Bill: colour details, sometimes shape.
Wings: colour of tips, colour of front edge, and the upper and undersides.
Tail: length in relation to the wing tips when at rest. Tail streamers (outer tail feathers) in terns.
Immature birds – are more difficult as changes occur in first, second and sometimes third years. Juvenile birds are speckled brown and have a dark band across the tip of the tail.
The Gulls to expect and their identifying points:–
Blackhead Gull:
Wings: white front edge on upper wing, black tips not noticeable.
Head: dark brown in summer, only a dark spot behind the eye in winter.
Legs and bill: dark red.
Common Gull:
Wings: black tips with white spots. White rear edge.
Legs: pale greenish-yellow.
Bill: yellow.
Herring Gull:
Wings: as Common Gull, but underwing dark tip.
Size: larger than the other gulls except the Blackbacks.
Legs: flesh pink.
Bill: yellow with red patch on tip of the lower half.

Greater Blackbacked Gull:
Size: largest gull.
Back: black.
Black wings: white rear edge. Dark flight feathers on the underside.
Bill: as Herring Gull.
Legs: flesh pink.
Lesser Blackbacked Gull:
Size: as Herring Gull.
Back: summer, dark grey (British birds); winter, almost black (Scandinavian race).
Wings: white rear edge, black tip and dark flight feathers on underside, project beyond tail when at rest.
Bill: as Herring Gull.
Legs: yellow.
Kittiwake:
Like Common Gull generally, except for wing and legs.
Wings: black tips with no white spots.
Legs black, bill yellow, both short.

Terns (summer visitors)
Common Tern:
Legs: red.
Bill: red with black tip.
Rather grey rump.
Underparts: white.
Arctic Tern:
Legs: red and shorter.
Bill: all red.
Rump: white.
Underparts: tend to be grey.
Little Tern:
Size: smallest tern.
Head: white forehead.
Legs: yellow.
Bill: yellow, black tip.
Sandwich Tern:
Size: larger, more lanky or thin appearance.
Head: shaggy crest on back of head.
Legs: black.
Bill: black with yellow tip.

Terns
Sandwich
Common
Arctic
Little

The medium sized gull is called the Common Gull. It is certainly not common on the shore but tends to be an "inland" gull following the plough and resting in playing fields.

The Blackhead gull which only has a dark head in the Spring, is our smallest and most common gull. The sixth gull, the Kittiwake was once restricted to the rocky breeding cliffs of northern and western Britain. Mainly an ocean going gull, the Kittiwake is a bird which has in recent years increased in numbers to the point of sometimes nesting on ledges of harbour buildings.

Terns are smaller birds, coloured like gulls, but more slenderly built with black caps and graceful if jerky flight. There are four terns that are reasonably common. They are the Arctic and the Common Tern, both of which are rather difficult to tell apart, the Little Tern is now endangered and breeds largely within reserves. The Sandwich Tern is the largest tern and is a summer visitor, like all our terns. All the terns plunge into the sea to catch small fish, particularly sand-eels.

Another bird that plunges into the sea for fish is the Gannet, a much larger bird, white with black tipped wings which span almost 2 metres. Sometimes numbers of Gannets collect offshore, diving from a considerable height into shoals of surface feeding fish.

The sea bird that spends most time on the wing is the Fulmar Petrel. It looks like a stiff, straight winged gull and is a superb flyer. Apart from visiting the breeding cliffs it spends the rest of the year scavenging over the oceans miles away from land.

UNDERWATER HUNTERS

Seabirds that feed on or under the surface of the water include several that are highly specialised in swimming under water to catch fish and other underwater creatures. Among such birds are the auks, the grebes and divers, various sea ducks and the cormorant and shag.

Like the gulls and the terns they all have webbed feet (the grebes have lobed or partly webbed feet). But the long wings, designed for sustained and gliding flight, that gulls and fulmars have developed, are not needed if fishing is to be from the surface.

The three auks that are present in numbers around our coast, the Puffin, the Guillemot and the Razorbill have in fact short, small wings compared to their powerful body structure and weight. These wings consequently must beat very rapidly in flight, but are used as flippers when chasing fish under water. They have strong legs and feet for a long paddling take-off from water. But there is no problem on land as they nest on high cliffs where it is easy to drop away and pick up speed. They also have especially adapted bills, each slightly different for their more specialised feeding. The razorbill's powerful bill enables it to crush crustacea and shell fish and the great parrot bill of the puffin has edges which stay parallel, linked by a fold of skin, so that it can hold up to 12 sand eels at once.

All three breed on northern and western coasts where suitable rocky cliffs are available. This is not quite so important for the puffin because it nests in burrows on the sloping cliff tops but the other two must have cliffs not only covered with ledges, but with ledges that slope inwards so that the one egg the bird lays does not roll off the ledge. The eggs

Puffins

Kittiwake

Razorbills

Guillemots

Eider Duck

CLIFF WATCH

Cliff-tops are fine places to watch birds in flight. Binoculars are needed. **BUT** they are very dangerous places. Never climb down a cliff.
Leather soles are slippery on short dry grass.
Only go with a companion and permission.

- Find a safe, comfortable spot from which to watch and stay there. Let the birds come around you.
- Notice the different methods of flying: slow flapping or rapid flight birds, gliding and soaring round. Compare different wing shapes.
- Watch those landing or taking off — from the sea, from the cliff face or from the grass. Look for 'braking' as birds land.
- A wind comes up the cliff-face. Watch how that is used by the birds.

- Watch birds on the sea and over the sea. From the height of the cliff-top you sometimes see more. Are birds resting, feeding, diving from air or surface? Time the dives.
- Watch for movements of birds along the coast. Some will fly high, some low over the water. Are they going the same way? Are different species going different ways? How do the movements fit with the tide?
- Try sketching: silhouettes from above or below are best to start with. Then try different positions in flight.

themselves are very narrow at one end so that if they do roll it will be in a tight circle. These auks are ocean birds outside the breeding season, in winter some dispersing as far as the western Mediterranean.

Although closely related to the Gannet, the Cormorant and the smaller Shag both catch fish without plunging into the water from the air above; they are equally effective but they dive from the surface catching fish by

Shag

swimming underwater with powerful webbed feet and a long neck and a strong, sharp-edged and hooked bill.

They are around the coast all the year, although the Shag frequents more northern waters. They are easily recognised as large, black birds usually flying straight and steadily not far above the sea or sometimes standing on a rock or post and spreading their wings to dry.

There are also marine ducks that dive from the surface and feed below, sometimes at considerable depths. The Eider duck, more exclusively a sea duck than many, is more numerous in the north and west where groups of the black and white drakes and drably camouflaged females can be seen diving in relatively shallow water for crabs, sea urchins and especially mussels. After the breeding season birds distribute themselves more generally off rocky shores.

In winter ducks like the Scaup, Goldeneye, Goosanders and Redbreasted Mergansers and also several Divers and Grebes dive for food in offshore waters.

Like the others, these birds are highly adapted too. Their streamlined shapes underwater and feet placed towards the rear of their bodies together with long, sharp bills make them into very efficient underwater hunters.

WALKING FEEDERS

Wading and probing, walking and grazing, and paddling and dabbling – there are three broad groups of shore birds that feed thus. They are the waders, the wild geese and some surface feeding ducks including the Shelduck.

Sometimes, in late summer, autumn or winter when the tide is out, the distant mudflats and lower shore are dotted with small scattered parties or large flocks of various birds. Apart from size they might appear similar and all doing the same thing – busily feeding while they can. These are the Waders, and in the way they feed they are very different.

Oyster Catchers

Redshank

They vary from the pale little Sanderlings dashing to and fro along the water's edge and never being caught by the waves, or the black and white Oyster Catchers chiselling and prizing open mussels, to the long billed Curlews poking and probing into the mud, often in quite deep water.

There are many more, each feeding in their own specialised ways; the Turnstone literally tipping over stones to feed on creatures hiding underneath, Purple Sandpipers picking out creatures among the seaweed covered rocks, and the Dunlins, a little like the Sanderlings but shallow probers into the mud rather than surface pickers.

There are many more probing into the mud, but look carefully, they have different sized bills and length of legs so that they can feed in different places at different depths for different creatures! These are the Grey Plovers, the Knots, the Redshanks and those with the longest bills of all the Godwits, Curlews and Whimbrels.

They are not in great competition and there is food for all.

Waders may be confusing at first, but look for the common species to begin with. Size will tell you that the smallest are probably Dunlin or Sanderling or perhaps the slightly larger Ringed Plover. Turnstones and Knots are slightly larger, but not as big as the Common Redshank which you will soon get to know with its noisy but attractive cries of 'tou-lou-lou'.

Equally noisy and as readily recognised are the Oyster Catchers or 'Sea-pies' as they used to be called.

The Curlew is the largest of the waders with one of the most well known and beautiful calls – 'curly-curly'. Its long curved bill is useful to probe deep but also to turn this way or that picking creatures from between and under large rocks.

Among the waders out on the mud and in the shallow water may be parties of some common surface feeding ducks such as Mallard, Teal, certainly Wigeon and maybe Pintails. However, most striking will be the large black, white and chestnut Shelducks. These are almost exclusively ducks-of-the-shore and are our largest duck. The shelduck

Common Scoter, a diving duck

Dunlin

Curlew

Grey Plover
(summer)

feeds as it waddles in the mud and shallow water sweeping its bill from side to side feeding particularly on a small mollusc (little more than 1 cm long) which feeds on the microscopic plants that teem in the liquid mud.

The largest birds on the winter mudflats will be the wild geese. The small dark geese are Brent Geese; these birds are the most common geese on the shore as they feed on a particular marine grass. The larger grey geese, of which there are four species, use the coast for safe roosting and resting on the mudflats or salt marshes between their feeding trips to large arable fields and pastures a little farther inland.

As many of the birds to be seen by the sea are visitors, either for the winter or summer or just passing through, what you can expect to see will depend on the time of year.

HOW TO WATCH

Waders, geese and wild duck are very difficult birds to watch. They are wary and shy, and they watch each other — when one goes they are all up and away.

To see them well requires binoculars: 8 x 30 are useful but 10 x 40 or 12 x 50 are better but heavy. In windy weather you should rest them, on your elbows.

If you can, study a map – an Ordnance Survey 1/50,000 or 1/25,000. A sea-wall with marshes behind, where few people go, is best.

If possible, make a reconnaissance visit to see:
● How far the tide goes out.
● Where the sun will be (you do not want it in your face).
● Where you can watch in comfort and shelter without being seen. (A spot behind the sea-wall with a broad view, or, where you can, from concealment, look down a gully or creek.)

● The best approach route that does not alarm the birds.
● Can you improve the spot with rocks or tufts of grass so that your head does not show against the sky?

Consider when to go:
● The weather and wind direction.
● The tide.
● The time of day.
Take a friend who is as keen as you. Make sure your parents know where you are. Take extra warm and windproof clothing in a rucksack and plenty of food. In cold weather, food, headcovering and gloves are important. Notebook and pencil will be needed.

Take your time approaching, and if the birds are disturbed for any reason stay hidden for a while. Look around with your binoculars, not everything may have gone and sometimes the most unusual will stay behind. Finally, the flocks may come back.

Never go out on the mud — it is much more dangerous than you think!

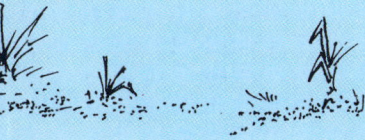

SEASONS AND TIDES

Peregrine Falcon

Grey Plover

Wigeon

Shelduck

Brent Goose

Living out on the sea or the sand or mudflats can be very hard – especially in the wind and cold of winter. But, whatever the weather, the 4 or 5 hours when the feeding areas are exposed and clear of water, day or night, must be fully used to gather food. In fact the more severe the weather is the more important it becomes to obtain enough food to survive until the next low tide.

As the tide returns birds must leave the feeding areas and, to conserve their energy, find somewhere safe to roost. Sometimes favourite resting areas are used by great mixed flocks of thousands of birds. These might be rocky islets or headlands, exposed islands or saltmarshes; sometimes during the lower 'Neap' tides the shore itself is still exposed enough to be safe. The birds will then roost there until the tide retreats again. Those birds with the longest legs, such as the Godwits, will roost on the side nearest the sea, while other species will each have their favourite parts of the roosting area. As high tide arrives they may by then be extremely tightly packed together. Obviously it is important that the flocks should not be disturbed whilst roosting because a great deal of energy must then be wasted looking for another safe place to rest.

The numbers of shore birds are probably lowest in the breeding season. As breeding ceases birds begin to move south, some British bred birds may move down the French coast to Spain or North Africa to be replaced by a population intending to winter around Britain which has travelled westwards from Siberia, Russia, Eastern Europe and Scandinavia, other birds may have flown south and eastwards from Iceland, Greenland and Canada.

Many of these birds may not stay with us for long. But our coastal waters and estuaries are important refuelling stops for birds on their way to southern Europe and the Mediterranean coasts or down to the coast of West Africa. Birds such as the Arctic Tern, perhaps the greatest of travellers, which has nested to the North perhaps in Iceland, will then 'winter' in the southern summer of the Antarctic. There is an instance of a young bird ringed in Britain and found six months later in Southern Australia.

From July until October great numbers of passage migrants arrive, stop a while and move on again. Many of these birds are juveniles and almost all birds will be in winter colours.

Keeping regular records and making systematic observations can lead to exciting discoveries when armed with binoculars in a comfortable position with a good view across the shore.

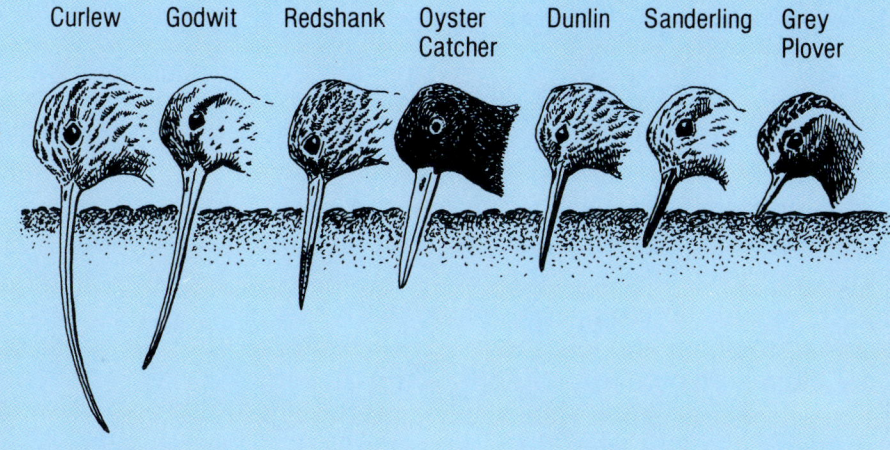

Curlew Godwit Redshank Oyster Catcher Dunlin Sanderling Grey Plover

- Spend a little while noticing what is happening. Are there any steady movements? Not just large flocks but birds in twos and threes, for instance are land birds flying in from the sea? Migration occurs like that sometimes.
- Are flocks of birds moving in one direction? If they are, is it a migration along the coast still going on even after the tide has changed?
- What movements of birds are changing with the tide? Is there a reverse movement after high water? Where are the birds going? If you can discover a roosting area, you can, on another occasion, conceal yourself before the birds arrive.
- Count the flocks that pass one point in each 5 minutes and estimate or count the numbers in each flock. If the flocks are too large to count then count 5 or 10 and then estimate how many 5's or 10's are in the whole flock. For very large numbers, flocks of thousands, estimate a 100 in 10's, fix that amount in your mind and then try to estimate how many 100's make up the whole flock. That sort of estimate is more accurate than a guess. Try estimating feeding birds as well as flying birds.
- Watch an individual bird that is feeding: how many times does it probe the mud before it gets something to eat?
- Record how different species are obtaining food, for instance, from the surface of sand or mud, from the edge of waves, from seaweed or rocks, from the mud or from water.
- Always note the weather, especially the wind. Which way is it blowing? For instance, a strong wind blowing towards the shore may force migrating birds to move along closer to the shore for shelter.
- In the spring or autumn carefully observe small birds in patches of sheltered bushes. You may find unusual migrants; especially after windy weather.

It is the return migration in the spring when the adult birds are more splendid – and easier to identify – in their breeding plumage. The spring passage movement tends to be shorter than the autumn one. However, it has to be precisely timed as the northern summer is shorter than ours – although food might be plentiful for a few months and daylight lasts much longer.

One of the great sights of the winter seashore and muddy estuary are the vast wader flocks, sometimes containing tens of thousands of birds. Most spectacular are the aerial displays they indulge in as they prepare to land at their roosts.

If feeding birds rise and appear to fly wildly for no apparent reason, then look around for a Peregrine Falcon. During times of passage migration and during winter, Peregrines will haunt the estuaries and shoreline preying on wader flocks.

Another falcon that frequents the sea coast in winter is the small but rapid and low flying Merlin.

Black-tailed Godwits

There are two other birds of prey that you should look out for over the saltmarshes in winter. Both have slow, flapping, broad wings, one, the Short-eared Owl, has a short tail and rounded head, and the other, the Hen Harrier, is a large, long-tailed, angular hawk.

SEASHORE FISH

Rocks and rock-pools fascinate people of all ages, so in the pools of the shore what fish can we expect to find?

We could say that the fish fall into two groups, those that come into the shore with the tide from deeper offshore waters to feed on other creatures and those that stay behind living between the high and low water marks all the time. Some offshore fish spend the early stages of their lives in shallow tidal waters and thus they are sometimes stranded in the pools as the tide goes out; such flat-fish as Dabs, Flounders, Plaice and Sole.

This is the period when one eye gradually moves around to the 'top' of their head because flat fish are really lying on one side. Beautifully camouflaged on the upper side, you will not see them in sandy pools until they suddenly dart before you in the shallow water. When they 'land' on the sand with one quick, wiggling shuffle they are gone, invisibly covered with sand except for the two eyes on top of the head.

Spotted Goby

Flounder

FISH WATCHING

- Do not blunder straight into a pool with a net – it is wise to find a place to sit where you can see without the sun being reflected into your eyes and without your shadow falling across the pool. Polaroid sunglasses will reduce surface reflections.
- By keeping low as you approach and moving very slowly you will not cause a panic in the pool. Remember, fish looking up will see you silhouetted against the sky. Binoculars may be useful if you are not too close and the magnification is not too great.
- If, after watching several minutes, you see no movement anywhere, try carefully dropping a small piece of food into the pool – a piece of meat, raw fish or crushed winkle. Remember, move slowly and now watch for the 'scent message' to get round the pool.
- After your 'watch' you may wish to explore, quietly and gently, by feeling under the seaweed and rocks; you may then cause something to emerge but have a net or large container full of weed ready in place, because the fugitive will look for another dark weedy place in which to hide!
- If you are going to collect fish for an aquarium which you have **already** set-up (see page 29), remember that even a large aquarium can only hold a few fish in a healthy condition. Take only small specimens and only one or two of each kind. Return them to the place where you found them when you no longer wish to watch them at home.
- The following are suitable species:– The Common Blenny, or the Spotted Goby which is probably the best of the goby family as it will be more active; the Sea Scorpion can be kept also but may take a while to settle down. Butterfish and Rocklings are also suitable.

Young eels (15–20 cms) can often be found in rock pools especially if there is nearby a stream or river entering the sea. Sand eels, not eels but long narrow fish, are sometimes found in the lower pools buried in the sand and waiting for the return of the tide.

Most specialised, and the ones you are more likely to find in pools, are 'shore' fish, the ones that stay even when the tide goes out, like the Blennies, Gobies, Rocklings and Sea Scorpions.

A very common and, perhaps, the smallest (2.5 cm), shore fish is the Goby, of which there are several different kinds, but four that are common. These fish have developed a small fan-shaped sucker from the pelvic fins. Like a lot of shore fish they have their eyes right on the top of their heads. The Common or Sand Goby will hide in the bottom of sandy pools with just the eyes showing like the flat fish. It does not really need to do this as the colouring is perfectly camouflaged with the sand. However, when the sun shines on a shallow, sandy pool its shadow gives it away if it stays on top of the sand. Check how often it lands facing the sun! In estuaries the rather larger Black Goby is more common, while in rock-pools look for the Rock Goby which is also very dark coloured. The only Goby that does not prefer to lie on the bottom is the Spotted or Two Spot Goby; this fish swims among the weeds of pools in shoals.

One of the most common and well camouflaged shore fish is the Common Blenny (11–12 cms) – often called a Shanny. It is quite a bold fish that has a very flat face and thick, pale lips. Another blenny that looks much more eel-like is the Gunnel or Butterfish, so named because it is extremely slippery and difficult to hold. Most of them have 10 to 12 dark spots along their sides which make them easy to recognise. Rocklings are also eel-like. There are two species, the Three Bearded Rockling and the Five Bearded Rockling; they have three and five barbels or 'feelers' respectively on the front of their heads.

Also hiding under rocks is the harmless but most ferocious looking Sea Scorpion. It is another beautifully camouflaged fish that lies in wait and snaps up passing prey. Equally spiny but with quite dangerous poisonous spines on its back is the Weaver fish. Feeding on shrimps it will burrow into the sand with only its eyes, mouth and the poisonous spines showing. If 'stung' in the foot by these spines the very painful effect can be lessened by applying heat, for instance a hot water (or tea!) poultice.

Five-bearded Rockling

Sea Scorpion

Weever

SURVIVAL PROBLEMS

Whichever kind of seashore you explore, sandy, muddy, shingle or rocks, creatures will be affected twice a day by tidal change and on each shore they will avoid the effects of this in different ways.

On all types of shore there is the problem of surviving the drying effects of sun and wind (dessication). The second problem is counteracting the effects of wave action. Finally, to varying extents on all shores, creatures are exposed to a different army of enemies from those they had when covered with water.

A sandy beach might appear almost a desert – whether the tide is in or out – there is little or no plant life, therefore nothing to cling to. So for animal life the amount of wave action is a major factor. However there are some worms and shell fish that can remain buried and still feed by pushing themselves or a tube up to filter food from the water. On a sheltered sandy beach there will be a thin layer of sediment deposited on the surface and as this will contain organic matter there will be creatures able to survive on it; these are *deposit-feeders* that collect their food from the surface rather than that suspended in the water.

The deposit-feeders will include worms that can remain anchored in a tube but then emerge and feed on the surface around the entrance.

There will also be carnivores and scavengers other than the fish. Carnivorous worms and shell fish, scavenging shrimps, crabs and starfish, but they all need somewhere to go when the tide goes out so on sandy shores they must have the ability to burrow.

On muddy shores, and these are formed where the waters are relatively still in wide estuaries or behind sand or shingle banks, the particles that make up the mud are so small that suffocation – lack of air – is the problem. The mud will settle with a lot of organic matter that was until then in suspension. This will decay below the surface of the mud and accounts for the change of colour to dark grey or black and for the distinctive smell!

Shrimp

Limpet

Barnacles

Beadlet Anemone

Netted Dog Whelk

Thus on muddy shores there is a rich supply of food in the water and a rich surface layer. Most of the creatures feeding on the mud are mud-eaters; that is, the organic rich mud is taken in, the food removed or digested and the mud passed out of the body.

WHERE TO LOOK AND SEARCH

The safest way to explore is to follow the tide as it goes out; this is also the way you are likely to see more. Later, after sun and wind have warmed the pools or dried the seaweed and rocks, creatures will have hidden themselves or have become still and inactive as the warmer water cannot hold so much oxygen.

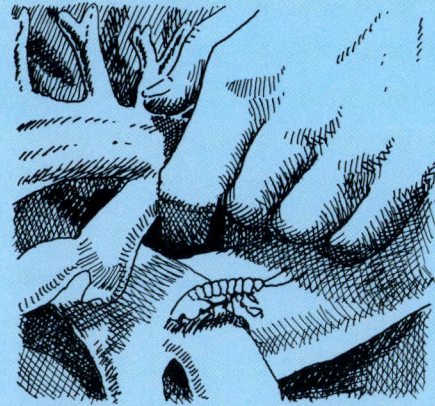

- It is well worth examining the 'strand'-lines – the line of weed and debris marking previous high tides. Turn over seaweeds and large pieces of wood for creatures will be hiding underneath!
- Look at the scaly patches of colour – yellow, orange, grey and black – on the rocks in the 'splash' zone above the high tide line. These are lichens – primitive plants able to withstand dry, salty conditions.
- As more rocks and pools are uncovered examine the seaweeds, look under them, look into narrow cracks in the rocks. Look into holes in rocks, some may be 'drilled' and round and occupied – empty shells may be 'occupied' too.
- Look on the lower surfaces of rocks and turn some over carefully. IT IS ESSENTIAL that you replace them exactly as you find them otherwise the creatures that live on them as well as those that live under them will die!
- On sandy shores, breakwaters, piers and posts may be the only things to which seaweed and life can attach themselves. Look in the little pools at the foot of posts and groynes.
- Dig into the sand where worm castings suggest there is life. Wash some sand from the bottom of a pool through a coarse sieve. With a finer sieve do the same with mud.
- Look in the pools on the lower part of the beach – they will be very different from those higher up. Take care to do it on a calm day if you are near low tide mark – some pools may be deep and dangerous!
- In calm conditions look at mussel beds and rocks on headlands. Life there may be exposed to strong water movement when the tide is higher, but filter-feeders and anemones will be able to obtain more food.
- Compare the rocks on one side of a bay with those on the other side for the conditions are probably very different as they face opposite directions – think of tide, sun, wind and waves.
- On muddy shores examine any stones or bundles of mussels that, being the only solid objects to cling to or hide under, will have attracted life. Look inside the tangled 'roots' or **holdfasts** of the long oarweeds near low tide line.

ALWAYS TAKE CARE, WEAR SHOES, LEAVE BEFORE THE TIDE TURNS.

Fan-worms in tubes

Sea Snail

The shore which is most devoid of life is a shingle or stony shore. Water movement is strong, thus no sand has settled and anything living is liable to be crushed as the stones are thrown or rolled about.

Conditions on rocky shores are the most varied, water will be trapped in pools and the rocks will provide a strong anchorage for plants and animals. When the tide is out the waving 'forests' of seaweed, which abound with life when covered with water, become flat, damp mats over the rocks but offering protection from sun and wind as well as from predators.

The pools, of course, provide another means of remaining wet and protected in hiding places.

Each large rock will itself contain a variety of life. Acorn barnacles may live on the top and upper sides, seaweeds, limpets and other shell fish can live on the damper lower areas. Among the seaweeds others can shelter and at the base and underneath there is safety for still more creatures.

Shores vary greatly and the highly adaptable life that lives there varies also according to the conditions.

CRUSTY CHARACTERS

Crabs, lobsters, shrimps, prawns, sandhoppers, sea slaters and barnacles are all called *crustaceans*, this refers to their hard shells.

By far the commonest crab on the seashore is a relatively small green one (up to 10 cms) called a Shore crab. It is easily recognised by its broad front edge with five notches in the edge of its shell on either side of each eye and three in between the eyes.

Hermit Crab and Anemone

To examine a crab hold the edges of the shell firmly between thumb and forefinger from behind. Turn it over and look at the underside. The plate of segments that folds round from the back edge is what is left of the crab's tail. The female's tail is broad and has seven jointed segments, the male's is narrower and pointed and has five segments. Crabs, prawns and shrimps are called *decapods* because there should be, including the pincers, five pairs of jointed legs, but often one or more legs are missing. If a crab gets into some difficulty it can 'shed' or 'caste-off' a damaged or trapped leg just beyond the second joint close to the body. Crabs, like all crustaceans – with a hard crusty shell – grow bigger but their shell cannot, so eventually they shed their whole shell. This happens quite quickly and immediately after the shedding the crab must grow rapidly, in fact it increases by as much as one third. The new shell is pale and soft and takes three or four days to harden. During this time the crab is very vulnerable to attack and must find a secure place to hide. If you find such a soft crab, leave it or replace it in hiding.

On the lower shore another smallish crab can sometimes be found, the Velvet Swimming Crab or Fiddler Crab. The flattened sections, especially the last, of its rear legs are why it can swim well. Its legs are marked with lines and at the point of the joints are bright blue.

You may find a large whelk shell *walking* about in a pool; this will be the Hermit Crab. A highly adapted creature that does not have its own shell, but rather a long, soft body, the rear end of which can grasp the inside of an empty shell to use as its home. As it grows it must find another larger empty shell into which it can rapidly transfer itself. The hermit crab has a large right pincer with which it blocks the entrance to the shell.

Shore Crab

Prawns, shrimps and lobsters appear to have ten pairs of 'legs'. Five pairs in the front, on which they walk, and five pairs of swimming 'legs' towards the rear. The first pair and sometimes a second pair in the front have small pincers with which the animal feeds. Prawns (up to 7 cms) are more commonly found in rocky pools and have a long 'spike', often serrated or jagged, projecting from the front of the head between two pairs of antennae. This spike is called a *rostrum*.

SEASHORE EXPEDITION

A certain amount of equipment is needed to explore the seashore. Such equipment should not be used for **collecting**. It should be seen as a way of obtaining a closer look and examination of a creature. Only rarely is it necessary to remove creatures from the shore. More can be found out by watching them in their natural surroundings, or, in a container before you return them to the place where you found them.
DO NOT LEAVE THEM IN THE SUN TOO LONG!

What you need: a large plastic bucket, a white or light coloured bowl (round ones do not 'slop' so much), some large plastic containers (1 litre ice cream tubs), 2 plastic sieves, like those used for flour – one large one with a coarse mesh and a small fine mesh one. Some plastic bags with ties. Avoid glass containers in case you slip.

Nets: four types of net are useful at different times:

1. A fairly small, round net for use in rockpools – it should be as strong as possible.
2. A straight fronted 'D' shaped net. Like a 'shrimp-net' for use in sandy pools.
3. A small, round net made from a lady's stocking or tights. About 30 cms deep with a round plastic container tied into the bottom. Use this to sweep in deeper water for very small creatures – the **plankton**.
4. A 'drop'-net. This can be round or square but should be fairly deep with string tied taughtly across the frame. Attach a cord as shown – lower this net into deep pools, and from piers and quays. Leave it for some time resting on the bottom. Then raise it smoothly without a jerky first movement.

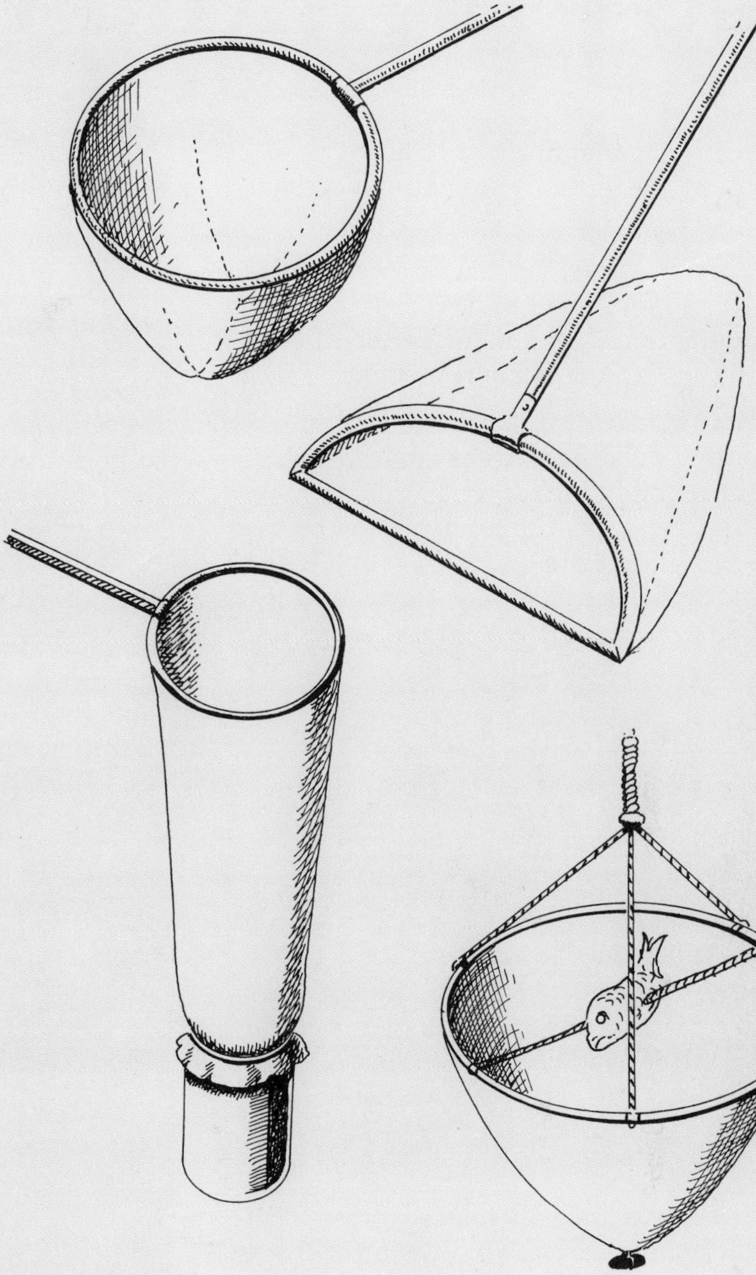

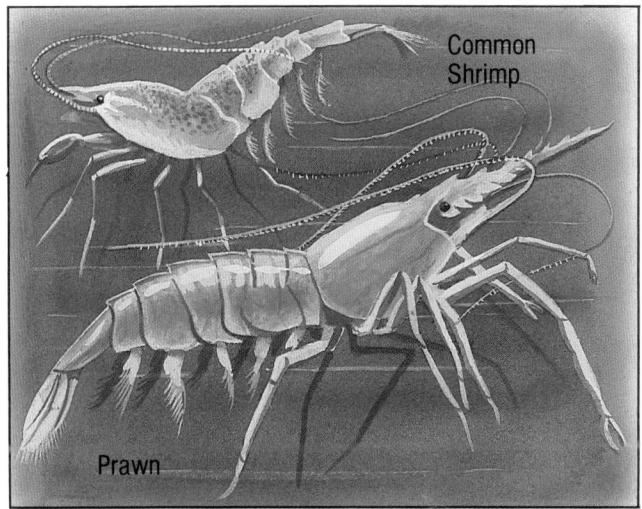

Common Shrimp

Prawn

Shrimps (up to 5 cms) are not as transparent as prawns but are speckled and spotted to match the sand in which they often bury themselves.

There are other crustaceans such as Sandhoppers, which you will find under seaweed along the strand line. Sea Slaters look a little like a woodlouse and are found in cracks and crevices.

Acorn barnacles are the most common crustacean, sometimes thousands cover each rock. Watch them closely when they are covered with water – look for the feathery 'hand' gathering in food!

FLOWER ANIMALS

As a means of camouflage or of luring food-prey within reach, many sea animals are so beautifully coloured and strangely shaped that to us they appear to be flowers rather than animals.

Sea Anemones are even named after a flower and one is called the Dahlia Anemone.

Equally attractive and as delicate as flowers are the Jelly Fish. Even spiky creatures like Sea Urchins and Starfish are hardly animal-like, while some Sea Cucumbers carry posies of 'flowers'. There are also worms that look like delicate daisies blooming in the mud.

Beadlet Anemones

The jelly-fish and sea anemones are very primitive animals. They are little more than a hollow body or pouch with an opening which is the food entrance or 'mouth'. The undigested prey remains are ejected through the same opening. When the tide is out and an anemone is exposed on the side of a rock it will be contracted and look like a blob of shiny jelly. Find one in a pool before it is exposed to air and it will have opened a 'daisy' of tentacles. If a shrimp or some other morsel of food touches a sticky tentacle other tentacle arms move towards the victim. Each arm is equipped with thousands of sting cells which when triggered off numb and paralyse the prey. The tentacles contract inwards towards the central 'mouth' closing around the food.

There are several different kinds of sea anemone, but the most common is the Beadlet

Anemone. It is one colour though this varies considerably, but it can be recognised by the row of blue spots, which show when the animal is half closed, between the outer rim and the tentacles.

Jelly fish are often found stranded on the sand. Usually they are the Common Jelly Fish and about 10 to 20 cms across with four purple rings in the centre. This jelly fish is rarely responsible when bathers are stung, but care should be taken not to handle the other larger kinds with longer tentacles as they can sting painfully. The tentacles are used to sting and capture live food.

Also found washed-up is the Common Starfish. It can vary in colour from orange to pink, mauve or red. The underside of each of

Common Starfish eating a mussel

26

Brittle Star

as they have small mouths, but the common starfish is a carnivore that feeds especially on mussels. It surrounds the mussel with its arms and the combined power of the sucker feet steadily pulling is so great that eventually it is able to open the mussel. The starfish turns its stomach inside out and inserts it into the opened mussel digesting the mussel within its own two shells.

Sea Urchin

the five arms has a hollow groove lined with little tube-like sucker feet. The 'feet' at the tip of the arm can 'smell' or 'taste' food and guide the slow moving starfish towards it. Very thin spidery starfish are the Brittle-stars – these must be handled with care as they can break an arm off quite readily. As long as the central disc is intact the creature can re-grow all five arms if necessary. There are several kinds and those occurring on rocky shores are quite small (2–5 cms) while on sandy shores there are larger species (10–30 cms). Brittle-stars feed on very small creatures or pieces of food

Sea urchins are closely related to starfish. They are hard, spiny balls with long 'tube' feet with which they move about browsing on seaweed, barnacles, worms and other small creatures growing on rocks or the bottom.

SEASHORE INVESTIGATIONS

It is often difficult to examine some creatures unless they are immersed in water and then a clear-sided container which enables you to look from the side is very useful.

● Acorn barnacles are best examined with a lens by placing a stone or a

mussel which has some barnacles on it in a container of sea water. After a while the barnacles may open and start feeding.

● Anemones are best watched – and fed! – in a shallow pool – but if one is found on a stone or small rock, it can be examined more easily in a container of sea water.

● If you find a washed-up starfish that is still alive place it in a shallow dish of water. Look at the tube-feet when it is upside down. When reversed again in the water, examine the upperside as the little lumps and 'pimples' on the surface are either tiny feathery gills with which it breathes or little short armed claws for removing seaweed, sand and debris that would otherwise clog up the gills.

● Pieces of rock and seaweeds which have hydroids, sea mats, sponges

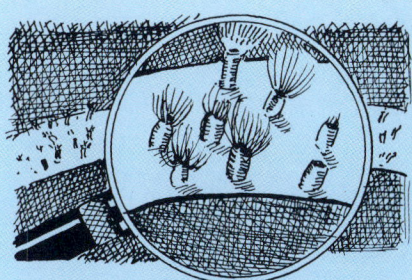

or white worm castings should also be examined with a lens whilst in a container of sea water.

● The movements of shrimps and prawns and even the inside of the transparent prawn can be best seen from the side in a shallow bowl.

● Keep the creatures out of strong light except when you look at them. If they are inactive try fresh cold water from lower on the shore – it will contain more oxygen.

BUILDERS & BURROWERS

Worms are easily recognised but those many kinds that occur on the seashore are sometimes strangely colourful and decorative, or they are rarely seen as they build tubes to live in.

There are two main groups of worms, those that are smooth and without *segments*, the Ribbon Worms, and those whose bodies are made up of rings or segments, the Bristleworms.

Ribbon worms are usually found on the lower part of the shore in the mud and gravel under stones. They are most easily recognised by the way they move. Swellings or lumps in the body move towards the head in a regular rhythm and the worm glides steadily forward. Some species are 2 cms long, others vary up to 30 cms, but a particular kind called the Bootlace worm grows as much as 15 metres.

The segmented Bristleworms occur in many forms but we can consider them according to how they obtain their food. There are those that walk, crawl or swim looking for food, and those that construct some sort of tube or tunnel in which they remain taking food as it comes to them.

Well known among the worms that move about are various kinds of Ragworms. Some are carnivores and others browse on algae but all have clusters of bristles on either side of each segment of their bodies which, besides providing a means of moving, contain the breathing organs or gills. It is these bristles along the sides that account for their name, creating as they do a ragged appearance.

The common worm called the Ragworm inhabits the middle and lower shore and like many others is a predator. It can grow to over 50 cms, but more usually is 10–12 cms. The mouth parts, armed with two hard, black pincer jaws can be thrust out to grasp the prey. Beware, they can nip fingers! Found on sandy shores are some that feed by moving through the sand. They are pearly white and called Catworms or White Ragworms. Others, called Paddleworms, are green or bluish in colour and swim very well as the bristle projections are paddle-shaped.

Sandmason Worms

Honeycomb Worms

Serpulid Worms

The commonest signs of worms on the shore are the piles of worm-casts pushed up by Lugworms. The lugworm lives in a 'U'-shaped burrow and thus a short distance away from every worm cast will be a small circular depression in the sand which is the other end of the U tube. The stream of water sucked in for the worm to breathe also carries sand and organic matter, all of which is eaten before being ejected as the cast of sand.

STARTING A SEASHORE AQUARIUM

Setting-up and maintaining a sea water or **marine** aquarium is not much more difficult than keeping a fresh water aquarium providing some basic rules are carefully followed.

- Sea water is more corrosive than fresh water especially on metals. Most of our marine animals require cool, well oxygenated and moving water.
- It is wisest, if you wish to use small aquaria, to use all plastic ones. A large aquarium can be obtained made entirely of glass cemented together, that is, without metal frames. Sea water reacting in contact with metal will cause poisonous pollution.
- A marine aquarium requires a good pump (designed for sea water) to aerate the water by passing air bubbles through a porous block. Aeration does not arise so much from the bubbles themselves but from the oxygen absorbed by the water at the surface if the surface water is kept circulating.
- A pump will also provide a means of filtering the water. As there are several filtering systems available a good aquarist shop will be able to provide all you require as well as detailed advice.

- Perhaps the major problem with any aquarium is pollution. Causes are usually overfeeding, resulting in decaying food, or the decay of dead animals or sea weeds.
- Coarse gravel should be used, spread 2–3 cms deep. Rocks, cleaned of seaweed can be placed to provide small caves and hiding places for shy creatures. However, do not create cavities in which decaying material can collect and watch the caverns in case something has died there.

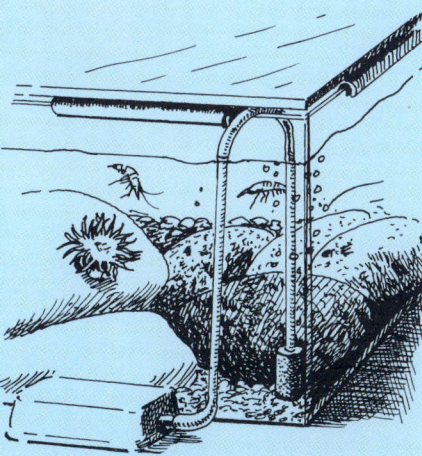

- Seaweeds will not survive in an aquarium, they will decay and pollute the water. Pollution has already occurred if a milky cloudiness begins to develop. It is wiser to watch for signs — if your creatures become inactive and sluggish do not feed them, but increase the aeration, circulation and clean your filter.
- Marine creatures do not like or require strong lighting. It will encourage the growth of too much algae. Switch on the lighting only at feeding time or when you wish to watch.
- A glass cover with short lengths of split plastic tubing clipped on the edge will reduce evaporation and escapes! Top up when necessary with **fresh water** — remember, the salts have been left behind. Occasionally fresh, clean sea water will enliven the conditions but first remove an equal amount of old water — preferably by syphoning the bottom, thus maintaining the same salt level.

Rules
Do not attempt to move the aquarium without removing almost all the water.
Feed no more often than 3 times per week.
Keep the tank in a cool, shady place. Do not expose it to strong light, shade the sides and back.
Syphon the bottom weekly to remove sediment which can decay.
Take care cleaning plastic aquaria, they can be scratched.

Ragworm

The various forms of Fanworms are far more spectacular but only when they are covered by sea water and they emerge from their tubes. These worms protrude a circular feathery fan of multicoloured tentacles which are breathing gills that also act as a filtering sieve. They gently wave food particles down towards the mouth of the worm at the bottom of the fan. The smooth leathery tube of the Peacock worm is made of mud particles glued with mucus. Fanworms on sandy shores use sand grains glued together, others use small stones and pieces of shell. The Stone-mason worm decorates the rim of the tube with a frill of branched tentacles made of sand grains. The Honeycomb worm builds a colony of sandy tubes often lying over a half buried rock on a sheltered beach. The very common chalky tube of one worm can be found on rocks and shells of mussels. It is triangular in shape, rather than round, with a point at the top of the entrance. Another form makes little coiled tubes like tiny chalky snails attached to seaweeds.

SEA SNAILS

One of the largest groups of seashore creatures are the Molluscs. It is the washed-up empty 'homes' of these creatures that are such fun to collect. You will know from collecting shells that some are twisted into whorls and others are in pairs or in separated halves.

The whorled shells belonged to animals called *gastropods* – a name that does not make much sense as it means *stomach-foot*. Certainly they have one foot, a body that is hidden in the shell and a head with primitive eyes and sense tentacles. They are obviously related to land snails and slugs. Just as land slugs have no shell so there are Sea Slugs without shells.

Common Whelk

As they have no shell in which to hide they are beautifully camouflaged and coloured. Others contain poisons and are brightly coloured as a warning. Most are vegetarians feeding on microscopic algae as well as some of the larger seaweeds. They have branched external gills – some of which look like bunches of flowers – on their backs. Many very delicate sea slugs living among seaweed are only 1–2 cms long, others like the Sea Hare and the Sea Lemon are as big as 10 cms.

There is one small group of sea snails that does not have whorled shells and these are the Limpets. The Common Limpet is easily recognised by its conical shell which it can clamp down hard with a strong sucker foot whilst the tide is out. This means it can avoid losing moisture and is protected from predators and the battering waves of the incoming tide.

Limpet

Netted Dog Whelk

MARINE AQUARIUM
WHAT TO KEEP
It is wise to keep shellfish such as whelks for a day or so in a bucket so that they have 'cleaned out' their inside.
- A few mussels are excellent as they are active filter-feeders and will help keep the water clean.
- Acorn barnacles on stones and shells are interesting to watch. Place them near the front where you can see them.
- Tube worms and Sea-Squirts, also filter-feeders, if you can find them attached to a stone.
- A few winkles will move about slowly browsing as algae develops.
- Prawns are good scavengers and excellent to watch.
- Shrimps will like a thin layer of sand in one corner but this may prove troublesome and become scattered.
- Brittle stars, small sea urchins and anemones – especially the Beadlet anemones – can be kept. However, the soft-bodied anemones may be attacked by carnivores.
- Common starfish may be kept for a short time.

Whilst it is covered by the tide the Limpet will wander off feeding on algae but usually never more than a metre from its 'home hollow' which it has ground out to fit its shell and to which it always returns.

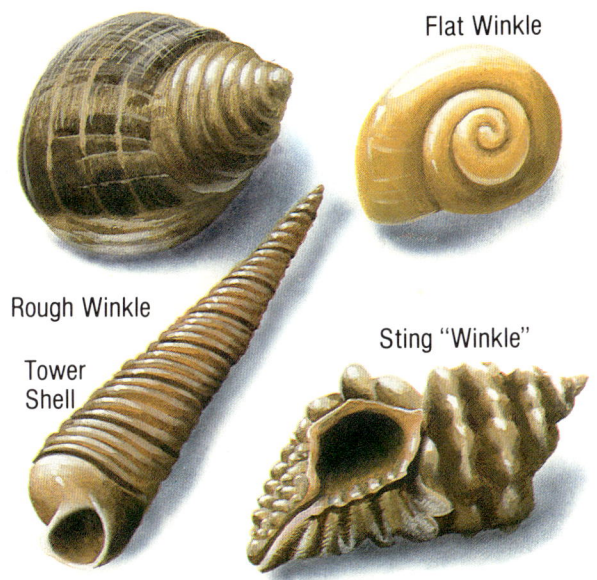

Flat Winkle

Rough Winkle

Tower Shell

Sting "Winkle"

The Slipper Limpet is a predatory shellfish that is increasing on our southern coasts after its introduction from America.

Painted Topshells – so named because they are colourful and look like a spinning top – are conical shaped and are the link between the Limpets and Periwinkles. They occur around the very low tide mark.

Although there are many spiral shellfish, the most elongated is the Spire or Tower Shell. It is the common Periwinkle, frequently shortened to winkle, that has the most well known shape. There are several kinds of Periwinkle but only four common ones and each of these tends to live on a different part of the shore. Above the high tide line in the *splash zone* living in cracks and crannies is the ½cm long Small Periwinkle. On the exposed rocks of the upper shore is found the Rough Periwinkle. On the middle shore the Common or Edible Winkle and on the lower parts under the seaweeds, the flat Periwinkle. The latter does not have a point on its shell and varies in colour – orange, yellow, brown, green–browns and even striped.

All these shellfish – like snails – have a rasp-like 'tongue' called a *radula* that scrapes or files food off the rocks.

Some, however, like the Necklace Shell, the Dog Whelk and the Sting Winkle (not a winkle but a whelk) are carnivorous snails that have adapted their radula and mouth parts so that they can drill a hole into the shells of mussels, limpets and barnacles and then eat the victim by pushing their tongue through the hole. The Common Whelk, a carnivorous scavenger, produces the largest twisted shell you are likely to find on the shore (up to 15 cms). Whelks have a long siphon or 'breathing' tube, like an elephant's trunk, which they can hold above the mud and sand through which they are crawling, and suck clean water to their gills. The bottom of a whelk's shell has a rolled groove through which the siphon can be pushed.

- Sponges and limpets do not last long and sea-slugs are not suitable either.
- Whelks will prey on other shellfish and should be cleaned first if you are going to keep one or two.
- One small shore crab will scavenge but may also prey on things like anemones.
- A small Hermit crab will be interesting to watch but it will attack some creatures.
- For suitable fish see page 20.

HOW TO FEED THEM
- Do not over feed – twice or three times a week is enough.

- Do not introduce too many creatures at first, and allow three or four days for a new aquarium to settle down after first filling it.
- Filter-feeders: a tiny fragment of fish crumbled near them or a small crumb of hard-boiled egg yolk (not too much!).
- A small piece of mussel or winkle can be gently dropped into the centre of an anemone. Alternatively, a tiny piece of raw meat or chopped and washed earthworm.
- Crabs, prawns and brittlestars will feed on the 'left-overs'.
- Small shrimp and prawns will provide live food for some

carnivores. Brine shrimps can be reared; purchase eggs from an Aquarist Shop. Instructions on rearing will be supplied.
- Remove uneaten food each day. Occasionally gently stir the water, this will increase food in suspension for the filter-feeders and if done last thing at night will have settled again by morning.
- Do not use oily fish meat such as herring or mackerel.

REMEMBER
Do not over feed – occasionally miss a feed and everything will be even more lively the next time. The community will still be healthy after a week.

TWIN SHELLS

Most common of all the seashells washed up on the shore are those which were part of a mollusc called a *Bivalve*, such as the familair cockle or mussel.

The animal itself is enclosed within two shells or valves which are hinged on one side. Look carefully and you will see that the two half shells of each pair are slightly different in the details of how one fits into the other. The complication of the hinge, the number of "teeth" or projections is one way of distinguishing the different species of bivalve shellfish. There are two powerful muscles that can hold the shells tightly closed if under attack. Bivalves have no head or radula as in the Sea snails, but there are two separate tubes or one double tube which can protrude from one end of the shell and a strong foot which can push out from the other end. The tubes are siphon tubes, where the lower one sucks in water and food and the other pumps out unwanted or undigested food particles in the "exhausted" water from which the oxygen has been removed by the gills.

Gaper

Most bivalve molluscs live in sand or sandy mud where their foot can dig and pull the creature down below the surface while the siphon tubes push up into the water. The Cockle and the Razorshell are both animals that live this way. The cockle's foot holds it 2–3 cms under the sand and when the sand is covered with water the two tubes are pushed to the surface and seawater is sucked in containing particles of food suspended in the water. The food is filtered out by the fine meshed breathing gills and passed to the mouth and then the stomach. Thus the gills absorb oxygen and filter food from the water. It has been estimated that a cockle siphons at least 10 gallons or 22 litres of sea water a day.

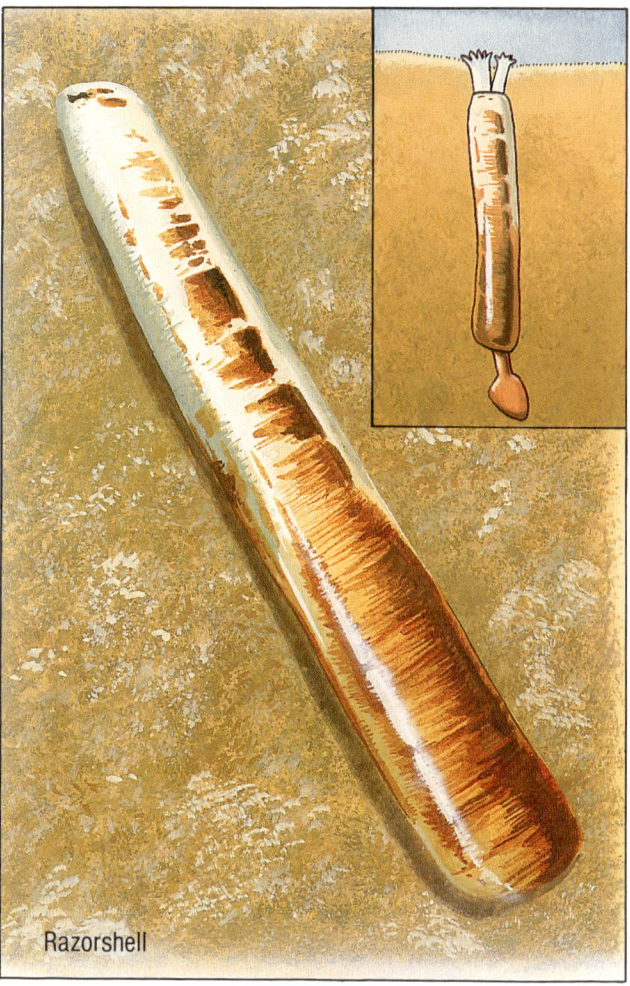

Razorshell

The Razorshell functions in the same way but it can withdraw from near the surface very rapidly by extending and expanding its foot downwards. Thus pulling itself, in its smooth, straight shellcasing, out of danger faster than a man with a spade can dig. The Razorshell is sensitive to vibration in the sand and the pressure of a footfall nearby causes the creature to shoot a jet of water up out of its siphon as it starts to pull itself down.

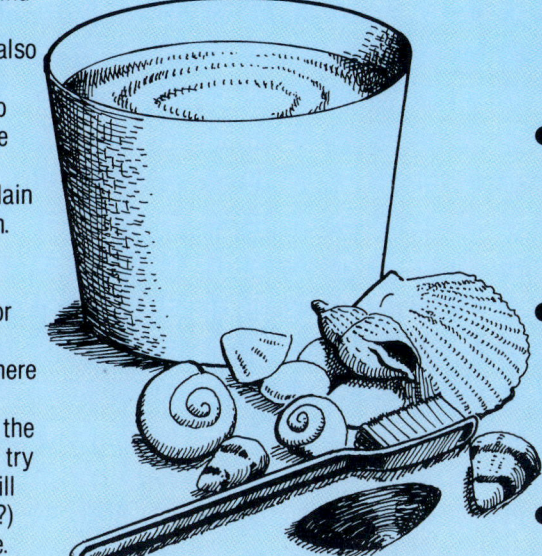
The Gaper, one of the largest shells you will find (15 cms long) has a siphon tube which allows it to live 30 cms down in muddy sand. The Tellin, one of the smallest and most delicate of shells which lives around the low tide mark and beyond has an extra long inlet or sucking tube because it feeds in a different way. Cockles, Razorshells, Gapers, Mussels, Carpet Shells and many others feed from food that is in suspension in the water; the tellin sucks up food that has been deposited on the surface of the sand or mud – it is therefore one of a number of *deposit feeders* that work as a vacuum cleaner.

Mussels

Cockle

The Mussel, although filtering food from the water, is not buried in the sand and its inlet and outlet siphons hardly protrude through the edge of its slightly opened shells or valves. It sites itself with other mussels in great beds where there is plenty of water movement rich in suspended food. It fixes itself into position with many thin, tough threads made from a liquid which hardens in the water very quickly. Many threads hold it down like the guy ropes hold a tent.

SEA SOUP

Many seashore animals and plants are fixed to a rock or buried in the sand or mud. Others have developed various means of "holding-on" and preventing themselves being thrown about by waves or swept out to sea by the tide.

The seashore has particular conditions to which shorelife has adapted itself and in those conditions these specialised creatures and seaweeds must stay. But, like the seeds of a tree, to survive successfully it is necessary to get away from the "shadow" of the parent and to colonise new areas. Seashore life of many forms does this by casting their spores, eggs, or their young offspring adrift in the waters of the sea to be washed up in a fresh location. The chances of landing in a place with just the right conditions are not very likely and the dangers encountered on the way are very great. Therefore, life must be reproduced by the million to ensure enough arrive at a suitable site to take up their fixed adult life.

Seaweeds or algae of all kinds free their microscopic spores into the sea, and they join immense populations of many different forms of microscopic plants already living there. This is food for millions of small animals. These small creatures are the young or the larval stages of crabs, prawns, shrimps, worms, starfish, jellyfish, sea urchins, shellfish and even the tiny barnacles. All these minute living things together are called *plankton*.

Although seas can be very deep, the teeming millions of tiny creatures and plants must stay relatively near the surface as they require light. Very little important light penetrates more than a metre below the surface. Thus most of this young life tries to stay in the top layer of the sea. Where currents bring minerals and nutrients to the surface the plankton is so thick – a soup of live things – that giant creatures like whales are able to gulp mouthfuls of water and filter out tons of plankton as food.

From the whales of the ocean to the filter feeders on the seashore the plankton is a most important food source.

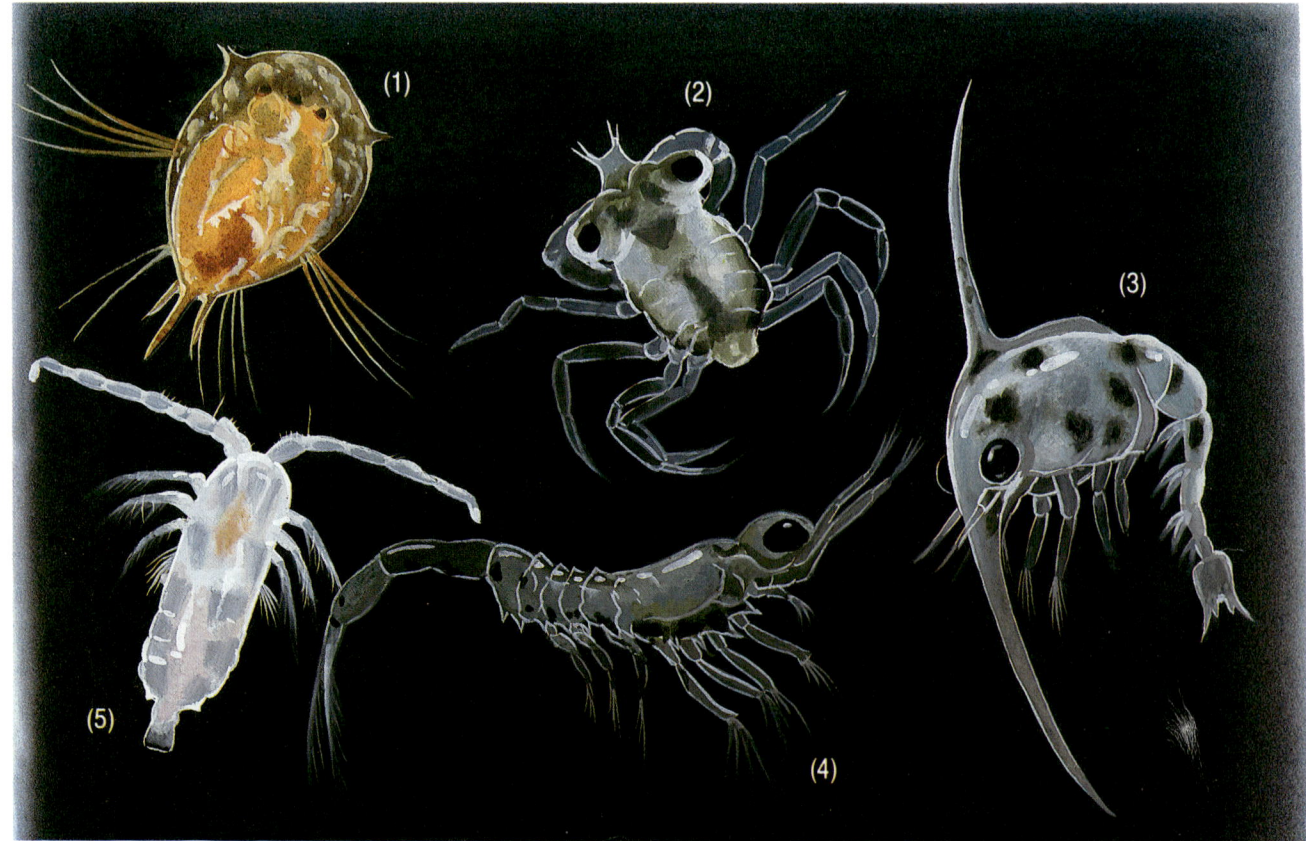

(1) Barnacle Larvae (2) Shore Crab Larvae – stage 2 (3) Shore Crab Larvae – stage 1 (4) Shrimp Larvae (5) Copepod

Besides the filter-feeding molluscs there are animals or groups of animals called Seamats, Seafirs, Seasquirts and sponges also feeding on microscopic food. The Seasquirts are little more than bags with two holes, where water and food is sucked in through one hole and squirted out through the other. Some seasquirts and sponges live in colonies. A colony of sponges may appear as a lump or blob of brightly coloured tissue encrusting the rock; the surface will be perforated by many small holes. Seafirs or Hydroids are miniature sea-anemones growing on stalks. These form colonies of stalks and become branched like small trees. Seamats are flat colonies of honeycomb-like cells each containing an animal. Each tiny animal in the lace work of cells pushes out a funnel of tentacles to catch food. All these animals, although looking like plants, "bud-off" or release, offspring into the sea to become members of the plankton too. The plankton is divided into the microscopic plants which are called *Phytoplankton* and the minute animal life called *Zooplankton*.

EXAMINING PLANKTON

- Explorer-sailors in recent years have tried using a large fine net trailed behind their vessels to collect plankton. They have experimented by using the plankton as food. It was easiest to use it as a soup but although very nutritious it tasted "fishy and slimy".
- It would be unwise to eat plankton from around the polluted shores of Britain but you can collect it and examine it in small dishes under a microscope or with a lens. Using your plankton net (p. 25) sweeping it to and fro through the surface water of deep pools at low tide, or trail a net on a line if you are lucky enough to be taken out in a boat.
- You will be able to keep some plankton in screw top jars for closer study if you avoid placing too much in one jar and keep it as cold as possible (even in a refrigerator). Do not leave it in the sun.
- The plant plankton or phytoplankton is usually very small and will be better seen under a

microscope if "lit" from below. Some members of the phytoplankton have beating hairs which help them float in the currents, others store oil or fat as an aid to floating.
- The Zooplankton, the animals, are also semi-transparent and can be examined in the same way. Some are the larval stage of molluscs, bivalves, star fish, sea urchins, worms and some crustaceans like barnacles which have been released as eggs and fertilised in the sea. Others, such as sponges,

crabs, prawns, shrimps, jellyfish and some molluscs like the mussel, hold on to the fertilised eggs and release the larvae into the sea. All these larvae are only temporary members of the plankton whilst young, for as adults they return to the shore.
- Other Zooplankton are permanently plankton. They are minute forms of jellyfish, sea slugs, worms and crustaceans including tiny shrimps like the Antarctic Krill that whales feed upon. These creatures spend all their lives floating about.

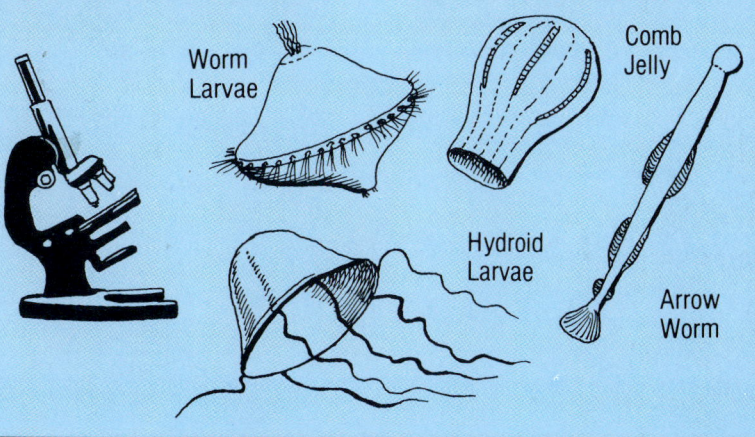

SEAWEEDS

Seaweeds belong to a most primitive group of plants called *algae*. The largest freshwater algae are small threads of almost microscopic size and equally small are the algae that grow as green powdery dust on the trunks of trees. Seaweeds however are much larger, very varied and include all the plants that live successfully in the sea.

For shore life they are most important as food and in providing shelter from enemies and the drying conditions when the tide goes out.

You may have noticed that the most common seaweeds are brown, or shades of brown from olive green and dark brown to gold. Some of these go black when quite dry. This group of common brown seaweeds are called Wracks. There are five main species and they are a very useful guide to use when exploring rocky shores because each one prefers a different degree of exposure to the air. Therefore they are found growing at different levels down the shore. Different creatures can be found inhabiting the different *zones* created as each seaweed is dominant in sequence.

Thong Weed

Channelled Wrack

Bladder Wrack

RECORDING SHORE-LIFE

- Aided by the wracks, you should begin by identifying the four zones, that is:-
a) the splash zone, which is only covered by the very highest tides
b) the upper shore, between the highest and lowest high tides and therefore uncovered most of the time
c) the middle shore – the largest area between the **Neap** high and low tides, which is covered and uncovered by the tide for about an equal amount of time
c) the lower shore – between the Neap low tides and the lowest Spring tide. That is, the area covered most of the time.
- Record the species of creatures you find in each zone and the numbers of species, for example the periwinkles, in a given area, such as a square metre.
- Try marking limpets or winkles with quick drying model paint or nail

varnish and mark the place on the rock too! Are they back in the same place after the tide has gone out again? Move them to another spot a few metres away and see what happens after the next tide.
- Check the temperature of pools as the tide leaves them and check them again every half hour. How do the upper shore pools compare with the lower pools? Do not forget to measure the temperature of the sea itself.
- Place seaweed clusters in a bowl of seawater and leave for a few minutes – see what comes out.

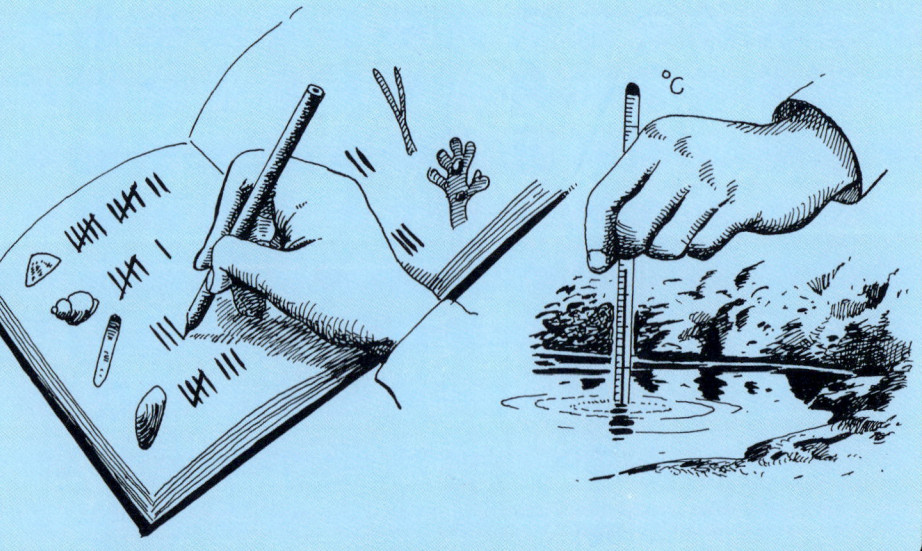

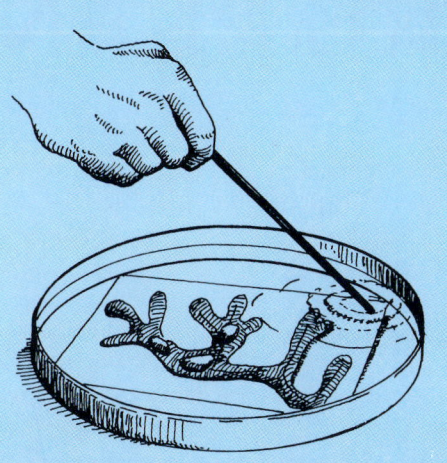
Starting at the top, at the highest tide line and in the area above that is called the *Splash zone*, is the comparatively small Channelled Wrack. So-called because the fronds tend to roll themselves around a central groove that runs down each one and thus delaying the process of drying out.

Below the high tide lines and the zone of the Channelled Wrack, grows the Flat Wrack or Spiral Wrack which is also sometimes called the Twisted Wrack. Although these names appear contradictory it is called flat because it does not have bladders, and twisted because the fronds tend to curl. This wrack is dominant on the upper shore.

The larger middle shore zone on a sheltered shore can be identified by looking for the Knotted Wrack. This is recognised by the narrow fronds with large single and very tough bladders. Also in the middle zone can be found the Bladder Wrack, which has pairs of bladders on broad fronds, that can be popped by squeezing. This common wrack is found on more exposed shores than the knotted wrack.

In the lowest zone just above the low tide line occurs the Serrated or Toothed Wrack. It has no bladders but has saw-toothed edges to the fronds.

Apart from the wracks you will have noticed the Green seaweeds – one of the most common being the delicate Sea Lettuce. The green weeds occur in the pools of the upper and middle shore where there is plenty of light. In the deep and darker pools of the lower beach and below the low tide line you will find many of the beautiful Red seaweeds. They are adapted to use the light in the darker conditions.

At the time of the *Spring tides* (full moon and new moon), which are the highest and very lowest tides, the large brown Oarweeds or Kelps are then exposed with others such as the Thong-weed all of which ocur in this lowest and otherwise unexposed area of the shore.

This is an interesting area to explore – but take care for the pools and gullies can be deep. Seaweeds do not have roots but it is necessary for them to anchor themselves to rocks and they do this with a root-like *holdfast*. It is among the nooks and crannies of the holdfasts that you will find a variety of different creatures living that are only to be found in this lower zone.

Serrated Wrack

Sea Lettuce

SEASHORE PLANTS

On a sandy shore just above the seaweed strand-line of the highest tides, can be found the pink or lilac flowers of the Sea Rocket. This plant is often the first "land" flower on the sea shore. It is a relative of the garden Stock, the Cabbage and others of the large four-petalled Cruciferae family.

Like all the seashore plants, the sea rocket must be able to tolerate the most harsh conditions. It must withstand not only the salt of the sea spray, including an occasional dousing of sea water, but the wind that sweeps across the shore slowly covering everything with stinging sand, and the heat of the sun drying out every droplet of water that has not sunk deep down through the sand grains.

On a shingle bank, the Yellow Horned Poppy must survive the same conditions, and on a rocky shore Thrift or Sea Pink and Sea Campion may find even less moisture.

In the case of the salt marsh you may think there will be plenty of water – however, there may be too much and again it will be salty and the wind will blow just as strongly.

How do these many plants that are so colourful in July and August adapt themselves?

A lot develop fleshy leaves or succulent stems containing large cells in which they can store water. Some plants, like the Sea Holly have tough, waxy skins to prevent moisture evaporating from the leaves.

Thrift

Sea Holly

Yellow
Horned
Poppy

Sea
Campion

PLANT DETECTIVE

There are many clues to show how seashore plants survive –

- Examine Marram Grass, the tall, stiff grass of sand dunes, on a dry, sunny day. You will find the blades of the grass tightly rolled – look again after rain in moist conditions. Look closely at the underside of the blade with your lens. You can then see the corrugated surface of delicate cells through which the plants 'breathe' and which are protected from drying out when the leaf is rolled up.

Sand Sedge

Marram

- Also in the dunes, look for the large pink and white striped trumpets of the Sea Bindweed. On a dull day or as dusk approaches they will close up. It is a very deep rooted plant with small, round, fleshy leaves that store moisture.
- Try to discover how different species are specialised to survive on the shore. Ask yourself, are they:– fleshy, tough or waxy leaved, covered with hairs, deep rooted or able to grow new roots quickly?
- See how many new plant shoots you can count along one runner of the sand sedge that grows along the top edge of sandy shores.

To avoid being uprooted and blown away by the wind others grow extremely long roots reaching deep into the sand or rock crevices to find water.

Many seashore plants can grow in salt water conditions because they have increased their ability to suck in water but at the same time prevent the salt from entering their system by the increased internal pressure.

What about the blown sand that buries the plants? Those that survive and even thrive in the sand dunes such as the Marram Grass merely grow taller and develop new roots higher up their stem. Some like the Sand Sedge can quickly produce new plants in a chain along runners to colonise the new sand.

In fact, these plants, especially the Marram Grass are very important in *stabilising* the dunes – causing them to become firm by spreading their roots. While down on the beach the seaweed in the strand-line, together with plants like Prickly Saltwort and the Sea Rocket trap the windblown sand and form a row of hummocks in which the plant can grow higher and catch even more sand. This is how a new row of dunes can start to form. The bigger, older dunes, those farther from the sea where the sand has turned grey, can support other plants. This is because the older sand contains rotted plant remains and thus is richer and can hold a little more water. Consequently other less specialised plants are

Sand Sedge   Marram   Glass Wort   Saltwort

able to become established, and shrubs and eventually trees can grow. On the edge of the salt marsh, plants like Glasswort can colonise fresh mud and begin to trap more *sediment* with each tide. Muddy channels and creeks are eventually formed by the water draining away. Shrubby plants such as Sea Purslane grow along the banks helping to keep them firm and protected from the lapping of the water. Behind the banks of Sea Purslane will grow the Sea Lavender and the Sea Aster.

- Especially on a shingle shore compare the way various plants are growing with how the same species of plants are growing in a more sheltered position. Are they growing in a flat 'rosette' form or as a flat carpet of plants over the surface?
- Among the older dunes look for other species that are less specialised. Compare the total numbers of species of plants between the old and new dunes. Look in the old dunes for Centaury, Viper's Bugloss and Burnet Rose, for instance.
- Examine dunes for erosion by human feet. Look also for the large windblown gaps in the line of dunes. Have attempts been made to shield the sand with close fencing or brushwood? Has new Marram Grass been planted to stabilise the dunes? Great damage is done by the winter gales if the Marram Grass is trampled and cannot bind the sand dunes.

TIDE-LINE DETECTIVE

Even on remote coasts, miles from the ports or seaside towns, evidence of human untidiness and carelessness can be seen by the numbers of old boots, sandals, light bulbs, plastic bottles and other rubbish that is washed up on the shore.

The existence of this litter on the strand-line indicates sometimes the vast distances that the *flotsam* – floating rubbish – of the sea, is carried by the wind and currents.

However, the natural 'rubbish' that is washed up is usually much more interesting.

Most obvious will be the corpses of animals, and birds – sometimes even cattle, sheep or dogs – these can be a health risk and are best left alone. However, dead birds are less dangerous to us and are often dried up. Plumage details are worth noting on these occasions as future identification of individual feathers then becomes possible. Dead sea creatures such as jellyfish and starfish can often be found among the seaweed that piles up along the rim of the sea after a winter gale or a strong on-shore wind. After the heavy swells of bad weather many creatures and seaweeds can be found which otherwise live beyond the low-tide line. Great seaweeds like the long blades of the Kelps or tangled piles of the Bootlace weed are worth a close examination.

Among them may be not only many of the smaller, delicate red seaweeds but many creatures living on them. Small pale brown 'leaves' are commonly found – these are Seamats – colonies of animals – and if the debris is freshly washed up it might be worth placing the Seamat in a bowl of sea water to watch the tentacles of the little creatures emerge from each cell. An object like a pale, floppy glove, called Deadman's Fingers, is another colony of perhaps still living animals – tiny anemones in this case.

A pure white brittle piece of 'bone' is all that is left of a cuttlefish which is a small relative of the octopus. The 'bone' is really the shell of the creature which grows as an internal 'skeleton' inside the muscle.

Empty crab shells will be common. These are not necessarily the remains of a dead crab but the empty shell, shed when the creature needed to grow.

Whelk Eggs

Whelk Shell

WHERE AND WHAT TO LOOK FOR

- First look for tracks of creatures that may have been searching before you. Then look carefully before disturbing or moving the weed; there may be crabs, insects or other creatures not obvious at first glance.
- Others can then be found by gently turning the seaweed over and searching:
  a) Look inside shells and in the **holdfasts** of the big kelp weeds.
  b) Look for creatures growing on the seaweeds.
  c) Examine the sandhoppers and other animals hiding under the weed.
- Carefully examine lumps of wood or bulks of timber that look as if they have been in the sea some time.

You may find Goose Barnacles attached to the wood. If the wood has holes bored in it that appear to be lined with a white cement, this will be the work of a small mollusc, which is incorrectly called the Ship-worm.

- Little bunches of objects looking like small black grapes are the egg cases of the cuttlefish or octopus.
- Hollow round shells the size of a cricket ball that have a rough 'pimply' surface are sea urchins

that have had their spikes knocked off by the action of the waves.

- Look carefully as some collections of small objects may be seeds of seashore plants. You might try growing them.
- There will be many shells to find. Some, like the scallop, the oyster, razor shells and slipper limpet shells will have come from deeper water. The latter will probably consist of little columns of shells fixed on top of each other.

Empty whelk shells should be examined to see what is in them. The egg cases of the Common Whelk are frequently found. They are a creamy coloured ball of many egg cases. If each case has a small hole then the young whelks have emerged. Other egg cases often found are those of the Spotted Dogfish, the Skate and other Rays. They are roughly rectangular cases, black, pale yellow or light brown with long pointed corners or twisting tendrils that once attached the egg case

securely to seaweeds. If the case is slit at one end then the young fish have hatched.

In the Summer the tide-line is sometimes littered with millions of insects and insect remains. This usually occurs when a strong wind has been blowing from the land. The insects have been blown out from the land and, being unable to fly back against the wind, have eventually been washed in by the waves and tide.

Kelp

Bladder Wrack

Dogfish Egg Case

Crab Shell

Sugar Kelp

SEASHORE MAMMALS

Common Seal

Grey Seal

Apart from human beings and their dogs, mammals are not a very common animal on the seashore.

But during the night and early hours of the morning foxes scavenge even well used beaches and in more remote places they are a serious threat to ground-nesting seabirds and their eggs. Brown Rats are also a threat to eggs and young.

The more wild, undisturbed shores and estuaries are visited in winter by Otters and tracks might then be worth watching for.

A closer connection with the sea, however, is maintained by seals. On British shores two seals occur. One, the Common Seal, called the Harbour Seal in America, frequently hauls itself out onto sand and mud banks. If you wish to see this seal, the sand banks near the mouths of rivers and harbours are good places to scan with binoculars at low tide for the resting seals. The Common Seal frequents the east coast, especially the Wash and Norfolk coast, while the other seal, the Grey or Atlantic seal, is more likely to be seen on rocky western and northern shores, although a large population breeds on the Farne Islands.

Three quarters of the world's population of grey seals breed on the British coasts and they come ashore in the Autumn to give birth to their pups. The grey seal is larger than the common seal. The large bulls can be almost 3 metres long while the common seal bulls are about 2 metres. Size, however, is deceptive when you have nothing with which to compare the animal. It is the profile of the head which makes identification easier as the common seal looks rather more dog-like.

Seals feed on fish and shellfish and therefore are not very popular with the men who make their living from fishing.

Their forefeet have become adapted as fins and their hind legs are the backward facing flippers at the rear end of the body. They appear awkward on land but not in the sea, where their streamlined shape enables them to be very fast swimmers.

Do not attempt to walk out at low tide to examine distant sand banks where seals may be lying without an adult who knows the shore and is aware of the dangers of being cut off by the incoming tide.

Also warm blooded, air breathing and well streamlined by blubber are the other sea mammals, the whales, including the Porpoises and Dolphins that can sometimes be seen from the shore moving along the coast in their typical manner, breaking through the surface.

Dolphin

They are really small *Toothed* whales. The black and white Killer whale is also a well known member of this group which feeds on fish. The largest of the toothed whales is the Sperm whale which hunts deep in the sea for squid. The other large whales are the *Baleen* whales. Rows of baleen or whalebone plates in the mouths of these whales filter their food (plankton and small fish) as they gulp enormous mouthfuls of water. If you are lucky enough to see whales it is most likely to be off Scottish, Irish and the northern and western coasts of England and Wales in the Autumn. But occasionally individuals and even parties in the case of Pilot whales are stranded on the shore. When this happens the animal is helpless, because once even partly out of the water its weight is so great that its chest is crushed and it cannot breathe.

Seals, porpoises and dolphins are also occasionally found washed up as corpses on the shore.

BEACHCOMBING

Besides the living creatures found on the shore, one can find **inorganic** (non-living or never-living) objects.

● Much of the rubbish cast upon the sea by humans is inorganic. One interesting aspect of this can be revealed by examining the labels and inscriptions. A different language may indicate their country of origin. However, do not forget they could have come from a ship of that nationality passing by.

● **BUT** BEWARE of sealed or unopened bottles or containers. LEAVE THEM ALONE – they may contain poisons, harmful chemicals, or even explosives. DO NOT THROW STONES at such things. Report where they are to a policeman.

● Stones are inorganic and sometimes also have distant origins. They invariably show signs of wear from the sea – they are rounded and ground smooth by other pebbles and sand. Pieces of glass are also ground smooth in this way, although their texture is no longer like glass. Collections of pebbles will vary in colour, pattern, shape and the material of which they are made.

● Some pebbles, especially if limestone and from the beaches of Dorset, will contain fossils. Fossils are the harder parts of animals and plants that lived millions of years ago and became buried in sand or mud – the sediment of the sea, lakes or swamps – and which later hardened into rocks. These rocks are called **sedimentary** rocks. Fossils are usually of things that lived in the sea and sank into the sediment on the bottom. Fossils of shells are particularly common. But coral and ferns have also often left remains in the rock

● Usually the fossil is not the creature or plant itself but minerals which have been desposited in the cavity left by the original objects –

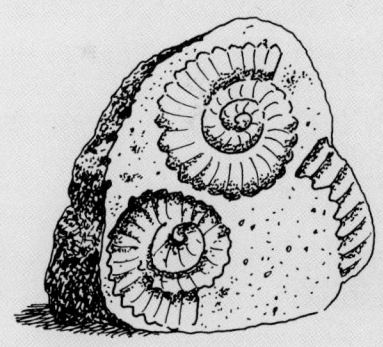

it is therefore a mould of the plant or animal.

● If you intend keeping the specimens you find, do not forget to label them.

● Cleaning, preparing and preserving your fossil is important. You should soak them in fresh water for several weeks to remove the salt. After they are thoroughly dry, protection with a plastic coating of some kind may be wise. Do not use acids without advice. There is a book called 'Fossils and Fossil Collecting' that can provide you with more information.

THE MESSY MAMMAL

Pollution of the sea and oceans by humans is a very serious matter about which many people, including scientists, are arguing.

Since the time of the earliest human beings the seashore has provided food, such as fish, shellfish, birds, even seaweeds. Numerous ways of catching fish have been devised, nets and lines cast from the shore as well as from fishing boats. Complicated fish traps were used and were an important means of obtaining food and a livelihood.

In this century, however, technical progress has been very great. Fishing and whaling are so successful, using modern technology, that populations have been greatly reduced and are, in the case of whales, in danger of extinction. Many fish are so scarce it is not worth trying to catch them.

There is now a great danger of disease resulting from the collection and eating of shellfish because of the pollution of coastal waters by sewage. Chemical and industrial pollution of the main European rivers entering the relatively shallow North Sea is also seriously reducing the stocks of fish.

These forms of pollution result from technological advance or population increase as well as carelessness. But there is deliberate pollution caused by washing out oil tankers

whilst at sea and by dumping chemical and radioactive waste, calculating that the resulting harm is acceptable.

Accidental pollution on a large scale occurs when there is spillage from wrecked oil tankers or oil drilling. The oil contamination causes great harm to seashore life and to seabirds, but, when used indiscriminately, the detergents that break up the oil can cause even greater damage.

WHAT YOU CAN DO

● With other interested friends you could consider your nearest coastline.
a) Decide what types of coast you have – cliffs, sand dunes, saltmarsh, sandy bays, holiday beaches or an estuary.
b) Examine them and discuss whether damage has occurred.
c) Decide what might be done about it.
d) Write letters to local councils, seek advice and offer help if it is required. There are lots of conservation projects, building paths, erecting fences, planting Marram Grass, building wooden walkways, with which you can become involved.

● A recent survey was carried out by the National Shoreline Refuse and Litter Survey, a Keep Britain Tidy group, based at 37, West Street, Brighton BN1 2RE.
● Why not make your own survey of the litter and rubbish on your beach and decide where you think it comes from?
● Try to find out whether any sea fishing occurs locally, either from the shore or from boats. What methods are used and which types of fish are caught?
● What recreational activities are there, and how might conflicts be resolved?
● Observe the Coastal Code and gently remind others – even parents and adults – when they break it. But take care to explain why.

Apart from pollution our increased use of the beaches and coasts is now causing other problems. Holidaymakers and visitors are often concentrated in places where access can be obtained by cars. At these places the erosion of the coast comes from the car wheels and from feet as well as from the waves. Once the shallow covering of plants and turf is worn and dies the sand is blown away and rock paths crumble and are eroded by rainwater.

Caravan sites are provided for the people who wish to come to the coast because of its scenic beauty, but often they look for the sandy bays where few others go and the paradox of many people all seeking isolation is obvious. Those enjoying numerous recreational activities with motorised boats and vehicles are in conflict with others looking for peace and quiet.

Obviously provision in appropriate places must be made for all. However, erosion of vegetation can be so serious that when the winter gales occur the coastal defences against the sea are broken by wind and waves, and serious damage caused by saltwater flooding and windblown sand.

Other conflicts arise over plans to reclaim big areas of salt marsh or mud flats for various purposes. Engineering projects can drastically change the flow of currents and scour away beaches or silt up harbours. The coast, then, is a very delicate and fragile area and its wildlife, which more and more people wish to enjoy, is under threat. The National Trust has bought areas of coastal landscape to protect it and has created safe long distance footpaths. The Royal Society for the Protection of Birds and many Naturalist Trusts have also bought land as nature reserves. Everyone should concern themselves with the problems while we still have some unspoilt coastline left.

Puffin – oil victim

SEASHORE CODE

1. SAFETY: The sea and the shore can be very dangerous.
   a) You should always know the state of the tide.
   b) Never climb cliffs or venture on mud-flats and sandbanks at low tide unless you have been told it is safe by someone who knows!
   c) Always obey warning signs and flags. Invisible currents may exist and waves during rough weather are very dangerous.
   d) Wind on an exposed shore can be very cold, always have adequate wind-proof clothing and appropriate footwear.

2. SEASHORE LIFE: With so many people interested in exploring the seashore, its natural inhabitants need protection.
   a) Do not unnecessarily disturb either birds or creatures living on or under rocks. Always replace any rocks that you turn over. Do not trespass on Nature Reserves.
   b) Do not collect unnecessarily – all life is best observed in its natural surroundings if possible. Many creatures take a long time to grow.
   c) Carelessness with motor fuel and engine oil can cause pollution and loss of life.
   d) Take oiled birds for treatment by experts!

3. COASTLINE: Protect the coast from damage.
   a) Observe restricted areas where grass may be regrowing and dunes re-establishing themselves.
   b) Stay on paths if requested to do so.
   c) Do not damage walls, fences or dunes.

4. SHOW CONSIDERATION for other people.
   a) Take your litter home, especially glass.
   b) Do not disturb the peace and quiet of others by loud noise or music.
   c) Park cars only in the places provided.
   d) Leave flowers and creatures for others to enjoy.

USEFUL ADDRESSES

Watch Trust which is really the junior section of the Royal Society for Nature Conservation (RSNC). There may be a Watch Club in your area. The Green, Nettlesham, Lincoln, LN2 2NR.

Royal Society for the Protection of Birds (RSPB) also has a junior section. The Lodge, Sandy, Beds., SG19 2DL.

The Countryside Commission: for advice, leaflets and pamphlets. John Dower House, Crescent Place, Cheltenham, GL5 3RA.

The Nature Conservancy Council: for advice and pamphlets on nature conservation. 19/20 Belgrave Square, London SW1X 8PY.

The National Trust owns and protects 400 miles of our most beautiful coastline, often containing long distance footpaths. 42 Queen Anne's Gate, London SW1H 9AS.

The Coastal Anti-pollution League: Alverstoke, Greenway Lane, Bath, Avon, BA2 4LN.

The British Trust for Conservation Volunteers have groups that organise practical conservation work. B.T.C.V., 10–14 Duke Street, Reading, Berks., RG1 4RU.

INDEX

A
Algae 34, 36, 37
Anemone cover, 22, 24, 26, 27, 40
Aquaria 20, 29, 30, 31

B
Barnacle, Acorn cover, 4, 5, 22, 25, 27, 34
Blenny, Common 4, 20, 21
Butterfish 20, 21

C
Carpet shell 33
Cockle cover, 32, 33
Conservation 44, 46
Cormorant 15
Crabs 24
    Edible cover
    Hermit cover, 24
    Shore 5, 24, 34
    Velvet swimming 24
Crustaceans 24, 25
Curlew 10, 16, 17
Cuttlefish 40

D
Dab 20
Dessication 22
Dogfish 41
Dolphin 43

E
Eel, Common 21
    Sand 21
Egg cases 40, 41
Eiderduck 6, 14
Equipment 25
Erosion 9, 10, 11, 44, 45

F
Flounder 20
Fossils 43
Fox 42
Fulmar, Petrel 13

G
Gannet cover, 13
Gaper 33
Geese, Brent 17, 18
    grey 17
Glasswort 39
Gobys 21
    Black 21
    Rock 21
    Sand 21
    Spotted 20, 21
Godwit, Blacktailed 8, 19
Goldeneye 15
Goosesander 15
Guillemot 14
Gulls 4, 12, 13
Gull, Blackheaded 9, 12, 13
    Common 12, 13
    Great Blackheaded 12, 13
    Herring 6, 12, 13
    Kittiwake 12, 13
    Lesser Blackheaded 12, 13
Gunnel 21

H
Hen Harrier 19
Hyroid 27, 35

J
Jellyfish 26, 40

K
Kelp 37
Kittiwake cover, 12, 13
Knot 16

L
Lagoon 10, 11
Limpet, common 4, 22, 23, 30, 31
Lobsters 24

M
Mallard 16
Marram grass 11, 39
Merganser, Redbreasted 15
Merlin 18, 19
Migration 18
Mollusc 30, 31
Moon 6, 7
Mussel cover, 26, 27, 32, 33

N
Necklace, shell 31
Nets 25

O
Oarweed 37
Oceans 5
Oil 44, 45
Owl, Short-eared 19
Oyster Catcher cover, 4, 6, 7, 16, 19

P
Painted Top-shell 31
Pebbles 11, 43
Peregrine falcon 18, 19
Pintail 16
Plaice 20
Plankton 34, 35
Plover, Grey 16, 17, 18, 19
    Ringed 7, 9, 16
Pollution 45
Porpoise 43
Prawn 4, 24, 25
Puffin 14, 45

R
Ray 41
Razorbill 14
Razorshell 32, 33
Recording 15, 17, 19, 36
Redshank 7, 8, 10, 16, 17, 19
Rocks 10, 11, 23, 43
Rockling, Five-bearded 21

S
Salt marsh 11, 39
Saltwort 39
Sand dunes 11, 38, 39
Sanderling 8, 16
Sand hopper 25
Sandpiper, Purple 6, 16
Sand Sedge 39
Scaup 15
Scoter, Common 16
Sea Aster 39
    Bindweed 38
    Campion 38
    Cucumber 27
    Fir 35
    Hare 30
    Holly 38
    Lavender 39
    Lemon 30
    Lettuce 37
    Mat 27, 35, 40
    Pink 38
    Purslane 39
    Rocket 38, 39
    Scorpion 20, 21
    Slater 25
    Slug 30
    Snail 23, 30, 31
    Sponge 27, 35
    Squirt 35
    Urchin 26, 27
    water 6, 8
    weed 24, 26, 27
Seals 42
Shag 15
Skate 41
Shellfish 22, 30, 31, 32, 33
Shingle 10, 38
Shrimp 22, 24, 25, 34
Star, Brittle 27
Starfish, Common cover, 22, 26, 27, 40

T

Teal 16
Tellin 33
Terns 12, 13
   Arctic 12, 13
   Common 10, 12, 13
   Little 12, 13
   Sandwich 10, 12, 13
Thrift 38
Thongweed 36
Tidal waves 5
Tide 6, 7, 9, 18, 19, 23
Towershell 31
Turnstone 7, 16

W

Waders 4, 16, 17
Water vapour 6
Waves 5, 8, 9, 22
Weather 6, 7
Weaver fish 21
Whales 34, 43
Whelk, Common 30, 31, 40, 41
   Dog 31
   Netted Dog 22
Whimbrel 16
Wigeon 16
Winkles 4, 5, 31
   Edible 31
   Flat 31
   Rough 31
   Small 31
   Sting 31
Worms 28, 29
   Bristle 28
   Cat 28
   Fan 22, 23, 29
   Honeycomb 28, 29
   Lug 28
   Paddle 28
   Rag 28, 29
   Ribbon 28
   Sandmason 28, 29
   Serpulid 28
Wrack, Bladder 36, 37
   Channelled 36, 37
   Flat or Spiral 37
   Knotted 37
   Serrated 37
Wrasse cover

Y

Yellow Horned poppy 38

PRINTED IN BELGIUM BY

proost
INTERNATIONAL BOOK PRODUCTION